CHARACTERS AND KINGS

A Woman's Workshop on the History of Israel

Part II

With Helps for Leaders

Carolyn Nystrom

Lamplighter Books Grand Rapids, Michigan
Zondervan Publishing House

Characters and Kings: A Woman's Workshop on the History of Israel Part 2

This is a Lamplighter Book
Published by the Zondervan Publishing House
1415 Lake Drive, S.E.
Grand Rapids, Michigan 49506

Library of Congress Cataloging in Publication Data

Nystrom, Carolyn.
    Characters and kings.
    (A Lamplighter book)
    Bibliography: p.
    Includes index.
    1. Bible. O.T. Kings—Outlines, syllabi, etc. 2. Jews—History—953–586
B.C.—Study and teaching. I. Title.
BS1335.5.N96   1984   222'.50076   84-27020
ISBN 0-310-41871-2

Scripture taken from the *Holy Bible: New International Version.* Copyright 1978 by
the International Bible Society. Used by permission of Zondervan Bible Publishers.

The chart on pages 20–21 is reproduced from *A History of Israel* (Second Edition),
by John Bright. Copyright 1959 by W. L. Jenkins and 1972 by The Westminster
Press. Reproduced and used by permission.

"Ezekiel 8" is reprinted by permission of *Christianity Today,* where it first appeared,
September 19, 1980.

Printed in the United States of America

85 86 87 88 89 90 / 10 9 8 7 6 5 4 3 2 1

CONTENTS

CHARACTERS AND KINGS

Four hundred years of Jewish history—that is the saga you are about to study. We pick up the narrative just after the death of the illustrious King David. The kingdom has expanded. Its influence throughout the region has reached its peak. The economy is stable. God-worship is firmly established. Patriotism is high. But David, a good king in spite of obvious shortcomings, is dead.

Enter Solomon—David's son and the first of twenty-two kings who will follow in David's genealogical line. These kings, along with scattered prophets, a host of kings from surrounding nations, and at least one vile queen, make up the characters of this narrative. It is no wonder that you'll need a chart to keep it all straight.

The complexities of the story will demand the reader's full attention, but the lively personalities of this era are worth the effort. You'll see Elijah, a fugitive prophet, hooting taunts at pagan worshipers while he humbly asks God to send fire from heaven to burn up his own small sacrifice. He got it.

You'll meet Jehu, who rides his chariot like a madman across the plains with a single bloodthirsty purpose in mind: to kill anyone connected with Ahab.

You'll know Josiah, the boy king, who turns his kingdom to God but can't persuade his own two sons, the future kings.

You'll visit Huldah, a woman prophet whom kings and priests consult when they need a direct word from God.

Four hundred years of Jewish history. Irrelevant today? Hardly. The apostle Paul, in his letter to the Christians at Rome, wrote of a giant tree with a grafted-in branch, that branch drawing strength from the deep root system of the ancient tree and bearing fruit for all to see. That grafted-in branch is the Christian church. Its root system? Judaism.

Thus, this ancient history of God's relationship to His chosen people becomes the history of all those grafted into a relationship with God through Jesus Christ. So Solomon and Elijah and Jehu and Huldah are not just amusing figures from a distant past. They are our history, our root system. We share their pain; we glory in their triumphs; and (if we are wise) we heed their warnings.

Immerse yourself in the characters and kings of Israel. You'll come out wiser.

Carolyn

BEFORE YOU CAME IN

Jezebel. Who's she? And Ahab and Elijah? Do you feel like you came in at intermission?

You did. *Characters and Kings, Part 1* came first. In it Solomon, son of great King David, came to the throne. He expanded the kingdom to incredible wealth, commanded honor from surrounding nations, constructed a palace for his one thousand(!) wives, and built a golden temple where his people could worship God.

Then Solomon died. And with his death came civil war: North versus South, Jeroboam against Rehoboam. And the mighty kingdom that had defended far-flung borders suddenly turned inward and battled itself.

Eventually, it formed two nations. The South kept kings from the line of David and maintained the holy temple. The North built alternate sites for worship. But the worship became, at best, a paganized form of Judaism. As for kings, the North took whatever king could most quickly kill off his contenders.

Then Elijah exploded onto the scene. This lion-fierce prophet ranted at the vicious northern kings—particularly at King Ahab and his clever wife, Jezebel. And Elijah carried the force of God behind his threats. Miracles appear rarely in the Old Testament. But at Elijah's word, the pagan worshipers saw everything from three-year droughts, to gully-washing rain, to fire from heaven.

It's as if almighty God, pained when His chosen people turned to false deities, gave them a shouted message—complete with visual aids—to make it easy for them to return.

Jezebel, queen of the North, opens Part 2 of *Characters and Kings*. Throughout her reign, Jezebel had encountered this call to return to God through the prophet Elijah. But to what effect? The first study reveals her character—and God's.

I'VE JOINED THE GROUP. NOW WHAT?

You've joined a group of people who agree that the Bible is worth studying. For some it is the Word of God and therefore a standard for day-to-day decisions. Others may say the Bible is merely a collection of interesting teachings and tales, worthy of time and interest but not much more. You may place yourself at one end of this spectrum or the other. Or you may fit somewhere in between. But you have one goal in common with the other people in your group: to enjoy studying the Bible together.

In order for you to meet this goal, a few simple guidelines will prevent needless problems.

1. **Take a Bible with you.** Any modern translation is fine. Suggested versions include: Revised Standard Version, New American Standard Bible, Today's English Version, New International Version, Jerusalem Bible, New American Bible, and New English Bible.

A few versions, however, do not work well in group Bible

study. For beautiful language, the King James Version is unsurpassed. Yours may bear great sentimental value because it belonged to your grandmother. But if you use a King James Version, you will spend a great deal of effort translating the Elizabethan English into today's phrasing, perhaps losing valuable meaning in the process.

Paraphrases like Living Bible, Phillips, and Amplified are especially helpful in private devotions, but they lack the accuracy of a translation by Bible scholars. Therefore leave these at home on Bible-study day.

If you would like to match the phrasing of the questions in this guide, use the New International Version. If, however, you fear that any Bible is far too difficult for you to understand, try Today's English Version. This easy-to-read translation is certain to change your mind.

2. **Arrive at Bible study on time.** You'll feel as if you are half a step behind throughout the entire session if you miss the Bible readings and the opening survey questions.

3. **Come prepared.** A small section called "Preparing for Study" leads off each chapter. These studies form a bridge between each week's discussion. Don't stay home if you haven't done the work. But if you spend a few minutes during the week on the "Preparing for Study" assignments, you will greatly increase the value you receive from studying *Characters and Kings.* Use the space provided in your study guide to keep a record of your findings. You may need to refer to it during your group discussion.

Some people have trouble concentrating on a passage of Scripture if they read it for the first time during a group discussion. If you fall into that category, read it ahead of time while you are alone. But try to reserve final decisions about its meaning until you've had a chance to discuss it with the group.

4. **Use your chart.** Pages 20 and 21 should become the most well-worn pages of your study guide. Check them

sometime during each lesson to see how your current study fits into the larger picture of Israel and Judah under the kings.

5. **Call your hostess if you are going to be absent.** This saves her from setting a place for you if refreshments are served. It also frees the group to begin on time without waiting needlessly for you.

When you miss a session, study the passage independently. *Characters and Kings* forms a story. You'll feel more able to participate when you return if you have studied the intervening material.

6. **Volunteer to be a hostess.** A quick way to feel as if you belong is to have the Bible study meet at your house.

7. **Decide if you are a talker or a listener.** This is a discussion Bible study, and for a discussion to work well, all persons should participate more or less equally. If you are a talker, count to ten before you speak. Try waiting until several others speak before you give your own point of view.

If you are a listener, remind yourself that just as you benefit from what others say, they profit from your ideas. Besides, your insights will mean more even to you if you put them into words and say them out loud. So take courage and speak.

8. **Keep on track.** This is a group responsibility. Remember that you are studying the books of Kings and Chronicles. Although a speech, magazine article, or some other book may be related, discussion of it will take time away from the main object of your study. In the process, the whole group may go off into an interesting but time-consuming tangent, making the leader's job more difficult.

While the Bible is consistent within itself and many excellent topical studies build on its consistency, the purpose of this study is to examine thoroughly a four-hundred-year stretch of Israel's history. Therefore cross-referencing (comparing a passage with other portions of Scripture) will cause the same problems as any other tangent. In addition to confusing people who are unfamiliar with other parts of the Bible, cross-referencing may cause you to miss the writer's intent in the passage before you.

One unique feature of this study, however, is that Israel's history under the kings is covered in two, sometimes three, places in Scripture. These parallel passages are listed at the beginning of each study. Feel free to use them to shed light on your discussions. They are different views of the same event and come from the same source: God.

Naturally, once you have studied a section as a group, you may refer back to it. Each writer assumed his readers would have the earlier passages in mind as they read each new section.

9. **Help pace the study.** Each study should last about an hour and fifteen minutes. With the questions and your Bible in front of you, you can be aware of whether the study is progressing at an adequate pace. Each group member shares the responsibility of seeing that the entire passage is covered and that the study is brought to a profitable close.

10. **Don't criticize another church or religion.** You might find that the quiet person across the table attends that church—and she won't be back to your group.

11. **Get to know people in your group.** Call each other during the week between meetings. Meet socially; share a car pool when convenient; offer to take in a meal if another group member is ill. You may discover that you have more in common than a willingness to study the Bible. Perhaps you'll add to your list of friends.

12. **Get ready to lead.** It doesn't take a mature Bible student to lead this study. Just asking the questions in this guide should prompt a thorough digging into the passage. Besides, you'll find a hefty section of leaders' notes in the back in case you feel a little insecure. So once you've attended the group a few times, sign up to lead a discussion. Remember, the leader learns more than anyone else.

ME, A LEADER?

Sure. Many Bible-study groups share the responsibility of leading the discussion. Sooner or later your turn will come. Here are a few pointers to quell any rising panic and help you keep the group working together toward its common goal.

1. **Prepare well ahead of time.** A week or two in advance is not too much. Work through the "Preparing for Study" section, then read the Scripture discussion passage every day for several successive days. Go over the questions, writing out possible answers in your book. Check the leaders' helps at the back of the book for additional ideas, then read the questions again—several times—until the sequence and wording seem natural to you. Don't let yourself be caught during the study with that "now I wonder what comes next" feeling. Take careful note of the major areas of application. Try living them for a week. By then you will discover some of the difficulties others in your group will face when they try to

do the same. Finally, pray. Ask God to lead you as you lead the group. Ask Him to make you sensitive to people, to the Scripture, and to Himself. Expect to grow. You will.

2. **Pace the study.** Begin on time. People have come for the purpose of studying the Bible. You don't need to apologize for that. At the appointed hour, simply announce that it is time to begin, open with prayer, and launch into the study.

Keep an eye on the clock throughout the study. These questions are geared to last for about an hour and fifteen minutes. Don't spend forty-five minutes on the first three questions and then find you have to rush through the rest. On the other hand, if the questions are moving by too quickly, the group is probably not discussing each one thoroughly enough. Slow down. Encourage people to interact with each other's ideas. Be sure they are working through all aspects of the questions.

Then end—on time. Many people have other obligations immediately after the study and will appreciate a predictable closing time.

3. **Read the passage aloud by paragraphs—not verses.** Verse-by-verse reading causes a brief pause after each verse and breaks the flow of the narrative; this makes it harder to understand the total picture. So read by paragraphs.

4. **Use the chart and maps.** This study is a history. Time and place are important to each event. Refer to them sometime during each study so that your group continues to see each episode set in its larger story.

5. **Ask; don't tell.** This study guide is designed for a discussion moderated by a leader. It is not a teacher's guide. When you lead the group, your job is like that of a traffic director. You gauge the flow of discussion, being careful that everyone gets a turn. You decide which topics will be treated and in what order. You call a halt now and then to send

traffic in a new direction. But you do not mount a soapbox and lecture.

Your job is to help each person in the group to discover personally the meaning of the passage and to share that discovery with the others. Naturally, since you have prepared the lesson in advance, you will be tempted to tell them all you've learned. Resist this temptation until others have had a chance to discover the same things. Then, if something is still missing, you may add your own insight to the collection.

6. **Avoid tangents.** The bane of any discussion group is the oh-so-interesting lure of a tangent. These are always time consuming and rarely as profitable as the planned study. A few red flags will warn you that a tangent is about to arise. They are, "My pastor says . . ."; "I read that . . ."; "The other day Suzie . . ."; "If we look at Ezekiel (or John or Revelation) . . ."

If this occurs, politely listen to the first few sentences. If they confirm your suspicion that a tangent is indeed brewing, thank the person, then firmly but kindly direct attention back to the passage.

A leader does, however, need to be sensitive to pressing needs within a group. On rare occasions the tangent grows out of a need much more important than any preplanned study. In these cases, whisper a quick prayer for guidance and follow the tangent.

7. **Talk about application.** Each study in this guide leads to a discussion that applies the point of the passage to real life. If you are short of time or if your group feels hesitant about discussing personal things, you'll entertain the thought of omitting these questions. But if you do, your group will lose the main purpose of the study. If God's Word is a book to live by, a few people in your group ought to be willing to talk about how they are going to live in response to it. Putting

these intentions into words will strengthen their ability to live out the teachings. The listeners will be challenged to do the same.

So, always allow adequate time to talk over the application questions. Be prepared also to share from your own experience of trying to live out the passage.

8. **Try a prayer-'n'-share.** Many groups start their sessions with fifteen minutes of coffee, then hold a short time of sharing personal concerns, needs, and answers to prayer. Afterward, the group members pray briefly for each other, giving thanks and praise and asking together that God will meet the needs expressed. These short informal sentence prayers are much like casual sharing conversation. The group members simply turn their conversation away from each other and toward God. For many, this brief time of prayer becomes a weekly life line.

9. **Enjoy leading.** It's a big responsibility but a rewarding one.

BIBLE STUDY SCHEDULE

Date	Passage	Leader	Hostess
	1 Kings 21; 2 Kings 9:30--37		
	1 Kings 22:1–40		
	2 Chronicles 20:1–21:3		
	2 Kings 2		
	2 Kings 6:24–7:20		
	2 Kings 9–10		
	2 Chronicles 23–24		
	2 Kings 13		
	Isaiah 6		
	2 Kings 16		
	2 Kings 17		
	Isaiah 36–37		
	2 Kings 20–21		
	2 Kings 22:1–23:30		
	2 Kings 23:31–25:21		

Names and Phone Numbers

PLEASE CALL HOSTESS IF YOU CANNOT ATTEND

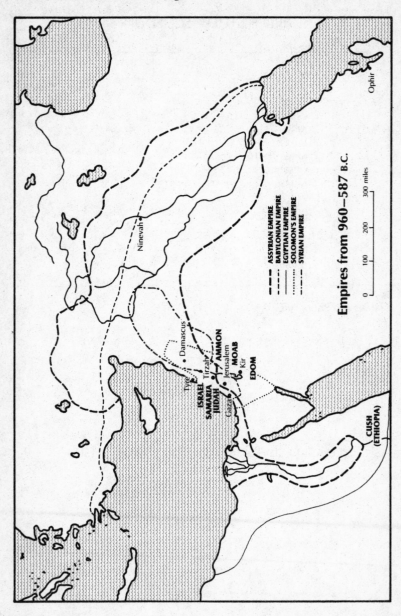

Empires from 960–587 B.C.

ASSYRIAN EMPIRE
BABYLONIAN EMPIRE
EGYPTIAN EMPIRE
SOLOMON'S EMPIRE
SYRIAN EMPIRE

0   100   200   300 miles

Ophir

Nineveh

Damascus

Tyre

ISRAEL
SAMARIA
JUDAH

Tirzah
AMMON
Jerusalem
Kir
MOAB

Gaza

EDOM

CUSH
(ETHIOPIA)

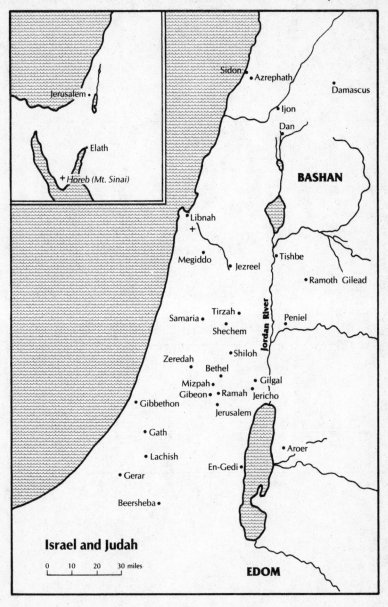

Israel and Judah

Jerusalem

Elath

+ Horeb (Mt. Sinai)

Sidon
Azrephath
Damascus
Ijon
Dan
BASHAN
Libnah
+
Tishbe
Megiddo
Jezreel
Ramoth Gilead
Jordan River
Tirzah
Samaria
Peniel
Shechem
Shiloh
Zeredah
Bethel
Mizpah
Gilgal
Gibeon
Ramah
Jericho
Gibbethon
Jerusalem
Gath
Aroer
Lachish
Gerar
En-Gedi
Beersheba

Israel and Judah

0   10   20   30 miles

EDOM

Year	EGYPT	JUDAH	ISRAEL	DAMASCUS	ASSYRIA
950	XXII Dynasty ca. 935–725	Solomon ca. 961–922		Rezon	Asshur-dan II 935–913
925	Shishak ca. 935–914	— 922 —	Jeroboam I 922–901		
	Osorkon I ca. 914–874	Rehoboam 922–915			
900		Abijah 915–913	Nadab 901–900		Adad-nirari II 912–892
		Asa 913–873	Baasha 900–877		
875			Elah 877–876	Ben-hadad I ca. 885–870	Asshur-nasir-pal II 884–860
			Zimri 876		
		Jehoshaphat 873–849	Omri 876–869	Ben-hadad II ca. 870–842	Shalmaneser III 859–825
			Ahab 869–850 (Elijah)	(Battle of Qarqar 853)	
850			Ahaziah 850–849		
		Jehoram 849–843	Jehoram 849–843/2 (Elisha)		
		Ahaziah 843/2	Jehu 843/2–815	Hazael ca. 842–806	
		Athaliah 842–837			
825		Joash 837–800			Shamshi-adad V 824–812
			Jehoahaz 815–802	Ben-hadad III	Adad-nirari III 811–784
800		Amaziah 800–783	Jehoash 802–786		
			Jeroboam II 786–746		
775	XXIII Dynasty ca. 759–715	Uzziah (Azariah) 783–742			Assyrian weakness
750			(Amos)		

Schism to Mid-Eighth Century

	EGYPT	JUDAH	ISRAEL	DAMASCUS	ASSYRIA
775	XXII Dynasty ca. 935–725	Uzziah 783–742	Jeroboam II 786–746		Assyrian weakness
750	XXIII Dynasty ca. 759–715	(Jotham coregent ca. 750) Jotham 742–735 (Isaiah) (Micah)	(Amos) (Hosea) Zechariah 746–745 Shallum 745 Menahem 745–737 Pekahiah 737–736	Rezin ca. 740–732	Tiglath-pileser III 745–727
725	XXIV Dynasty ca. 725–709 XXV (Ethiopian) Dyn. ca. 716/15–663 Shabako ca. 710/9–696/5 (?)	Ahaz 735–715 Hezekiah 715–687/6 701 Sennacherib	Pekah 736–732 Hoshea 732–724 Fall of Samaria 722/1		Shalmaneser V 726–722 Sargon II 721–705
700	Shebteko ca. 696/5–685/4 (?) (Tirhakah coregent ca. 690/89) (?) Tirhakah ca. (690) 685/4–664	688 ? Sennacherib Manasseh 687/6–642	invades invades ?		Sennacherib 704–681 Esarhaddon 680–669
675	Invasions of Egypt; Sack of Thebes 663			Medes	Asshurbanapal 668–627
650	XXVI Dynasty 664–525 Psammetichus I 664–610	Amon 642–640 Josiah 640–609 (Jeremiah) (Zephaniah)	Neo-Babylonian Empire Nabopolassar 626–605		
625		(Nahum)		Cyaxares ca. 625–585	Sin-shar-ishkun 629–612 Fall of Nineveh 612 Asshur-uballit II 612–609
600	Neco II 610–594 Psammetichus II 594–589	Jehoahaz 609 Jehoiakim 609–598 (Habakkuk) Jehoiachin 598/7	Nebuchadnezzar 605/4–562		
575	Apries (Hophra) 589–570	Zedekiah 597–587 (Ezekiel) Fall of Jerusalem 587 Exile		Astyages 585–550	

Schism to Mid-Eighth Century

Note: There may be slight variances in dates and spellings of names with the NIV, but none of these seriously affects the overall picture.

1

PREPARING FOR STUDY

1 Kings 20

1. Use your chart and maps (pp. 18–21) to see the relationships between the kingdoms of Ahab and Ben-Hadad.

Read 1 Kings 20:1–12.

2. Pick out Ben-Hadad's three messages to Ahab (vv. 2–3, 5–6, 10). In what ways was Ben-Hadad a threat to Ahab?

3. What do Ahab's responses tell about him?

Read 1 Kings 20:13–34.

4. Notice the purposes God gives for the outcome of these two battles. (See verses 13 and 28.) What do these purposes suggest about what is important to God?

5. What motives do you think Ahab had for making the treaty with Ben-Hadad?

Read 1 Kings 20:35–43.

6. What was the purpose of the dramatized parable?

7. How did God exhibit His trustworthiness to Ahab?

8. How has God demonstrated His trustworthiness to you?

1

JEZEBEL: ENEMY TO GOD

1 Kings 21; 2 Kings 9:30–37

"You Jezebel!"

The hissed accusation has resounded for millennia. A more disdainful denunciation is hardly possible. Who was she, this woman whose name besmirches history? And whatever did she do to win such notoriety?

Jezebel lived in the era of Elijah. On occasion, their lives touched—but always from opposite sides. Elijah was God's prophet. And Jezebel? Jezebel had set herself as enemy to God.

Read aloud 1 Kings 21:1–16.

1. a. Who are the main characters so far in this story? What can you know about the personality of each? _____

_____

_____

b. What can you know about the relationship between Ahab and his wife? _____

_____

_____

_____

2. Look up the Jewish laws of Leviticus 25:23–28 and Numbers 36:7–8. What reasons did Naboth have for not agreeing to Ahab's proposal? _____

_____

_____

_____

_____

3. What precautions did Jezebel take to be sure that her plot worked well? _____

_____

_____

_____

Note: Second Kings 9:26 implies that Jezebel not only arranged for the death of Naboth, but also for the deaths of his sons.

4. What does this conflict suggest about the values of each character? (What was important to Ahab? to Jezebel? to Naboth?) _____

_____

_____

_____

_____

_____

Read aloud 1 Kings 21:17–29.

5. What reasons did Ahab have to call Elijah "my enemy"?

_____

_____

6. a. Survey all that this passage accuses Jezebel and Ahab
of doing wrong. _____

_____

_____

_____

_____

b. In view of these accusations, what do you think Elijah
meant when he said, "You have sold yourself to do
evil"? _____

_____

_____

7. What exactly did Elijah prophesy? _____

_____

_____

_____

Note: For a review of what had happened to Jeroboam and
Baasha, read 1 Kings 15:29–30 and 1 Kings 16:7, 11–12.

8. Why do you think Ahab took Elijah's prophecy so
seriously? _____

_____

_____

The end of the story: Years later, Ahab is dead. His son, Joram, rules Israel. Joram is recovering from wounds received in a new war with Syria (Aram). (Remember King Ben-Hadad?) In this setting Elisha, Elijah's successor, commands that Jehu be secretly anointed king, and that Jehu begin to mete out the punishment God had promised on the house of Ahab. Joram's assistants quickly cross over and join the side of Jehu; they offer no protection when Jehu kills their king. (Joram's body was thrown into Naboth's former vineyard.) Then Jehu turns his chariot toward the palace of aging Queen Jezebel.

Read aloud 2 Kings 9:30–37.

9. How do you feel about Jezebel's death? _____

_____

Why? _____

_____

_____

10. Think back over all that you know of Jezebel. In what different areas did she oppose God? _____

_____

_____

_____

11. How might a contemporary woman oppose God in similar ways? _____

_____

_____

_____

_____

_____

12. Why is it dangerous to oppose God? _____

_____

_____

_____

_____

13. What does the story of Jezebel contribute to your understanding of God's justice? (Consider God's actions toward each of the major characters: Naboth, Elijah, Ahab, Jezebel.) _____

_____

_____

_____

_____

14. What might this kind of justice cause you to consider when you must make various moral decisions? _____

_____

_____

_____

2

PREPARING FOR STUDY

2 Chronicles 17

Turn your attention now from Israel, in the north, to Judah, the southern kingdom.

Read 2 Chronicles 17.

1. Look at the areas of Jehoshaphat's responsibility. Based on the content of this chapter, make notes on his performance in each.

   Spiritual leadership:

   Foreign relationships:

   Domestic affairs:

2. What advantages would having Jehoshaphat as their king have brought to the people of Judah?

3. Think over all that you know of Ahab, king of the North, and Jehoshaphat, king of the South. If these two kings were to come together, what influence do you think they would have had on each other?

2

AHAB: DEAF TO GOD

1 Kings 22:1–40

A commuter spinning the dial of a car radio catches a few words from a British preacher and quickly moves on.

Fingers groping for the hotel bedside lamp fumble across a Gideon Bible, then move on to the switch.

Eyes glancing from a passing car window spot a church on one corner and a Christian bookstore on the next. But the eyes remain outside each structure.

Christians have their own methods of tuning out God: singing an entire hymn without a single word registering in the mind; meticulously compiling a things-to-do list during the sermon; accidentally leaving a Bible at church and not missing it for days; feeling no compunction about a pattern of daily prayer long since abandoned and hardly remembered.

---

*Parallel passage, 2 Chronicles 18

There are many paths by which we can become deaf to God. Ahab's life (and death) warn us against such a route.

1. Glance back over the passages involving King Ahab that you have already read (1 Kings 16:29–21:29). What incidents help you define his character? _____

_____

_____

_____

_____

Read aloud 1 Kings 22:1–5.

2. a. What was Ahab's proposal? _____

_____

   b. How did the two kings view the project differently? ___

_____

_____

3. a. For background on the relationship between Israel and Aram (Syria), review quickly 1 Kings 20. Note particularly the terms of the treaty (verse 34) between Ahab and Ben-Hadad. _____

_____

_____

   b. Ahab is described in 20:43 as "sullen and angry." Why? _____

_____

_____

Note: Verse 2. "Jehoshaphat . . . went down to see the king of Israel." Here, as throughout Kings and Chronicles, people travel *down* from Jerusalem—even if they are headed north. This is because Jerusalem is at high elevation. To travel anywhere is down.

Read aloud 1 Kings 22:6–28.

4. a. List all the characters in this drama. _____

_____

_____

   b. Why is each one important to the story? _____

_____

_____

_____

_____

5. What was hard about Micaiah's job? _____

_____

_____

_____

6. Look again at Micaiah's statements in verses 17–23. What do these words reveal about the nature of God? ___

_____

_____

7. Look at God's law to His people in Deuteronomy 18:21–22. In view of this, why did Micaiah say in verse 28, "Mark my words"? _____

_____

_____

8. What did it cost Micaiah to speak God's truth? _____

_____

_____

9. What responsibilities seem to accompany familiarity with God? _____

_____

_____

10. Why do you sometimes hesitate to talk about what you know to be God's truth? _____

_____

_____

_____

_____

Read aloud 1 Kings 22:29–40.

11. Would you say that Ahab was cowardly or courageous? Why? _____

_____

_____

12. Look again at two summaries of Ahab's life and death: 1 Kings 16:29–33 and 22:37–40. According to these summaries, what is (and is not) important to God? _____

_____

_____

_____

13. a. Think back over Ahab's life. What opportunities did Ahab have for hearing truths from God? _____

_____

_____

_____

   b. In view of this, what do you see as the difference between hearing and receiving God's Word? _____

_____

_____

14. How might a contemporary person, with many opportunities to hear God, become deaf to His truths? _____

_____

_____

15. What precautions could you take to keep from acquiring this kind of deafness? _____

_____

_____

_____

3

PREPARING FOR STUDY

2 Kings 3; 2 Chronicles 19

This week your group will meet Jehoshaphat, king of Judah. Get ready to know him ahead of time by reading of two events during his reign.

Read 2 Kings 3.

1. What problem led the three kings to join forces?

2. Why did they call on the prophet Elisha?

3. What different parts did water play in this story?

4. What were the religious beliefs of each of the kings?

5. How did the other two kings benefit from Jehoshaphat's spiritual perspective?

Read 2 Chronicles 19.

6. In what situations do you have to act as a judge?

7. What were the judge's and priest's work under Jehoshaphat?

8. What reasons did Jehoshaphat give these leaders to perform their jobs in a responsible manner?

9. If you were to follow these same principles in situations where you must be the judge, what changes would you need to make?

3

JEHOSHAPHAT: BATTLE WEARY

2 Chronicles 20:1–21:3*

Battles in Jehoshaphat's life took the form of armies marching across the Palestinian wilderness: bloody conflicts in the valleys; hunting and hiding in the mountains. A whole city or kingdom could rise or fall on the outcome.

But battles for a suburban homemaker are of a different kind. My battles are often battles of time: four children, seven music lessons a week, countless ensemble rehearsals for the girls, sports practices for the boys, two weekly Bible studies, a prayer group, a seventy-family Sunday school to superintend, a weepy neighbor to console, music practice to oversee ("No, a dotted half gets three beats"), homework to enforce ("It can't be another spelling-review week already!"), a neglected manuscript scattered over the dining-room table.

My tired eyes meet my husband's across the supper table

*Parallel passage, 1 Kings 22:41–50

(noisy children spread out between). His eyes are equally tired after another day in his seventeen years of teaching math to reluctant seventh graders in an overcrowded classroom. The phone jangles in the background, but neither of us moves. We are battle weary.

I once experienced God's momentary deliverance from this battle. It took the form of a Midwestern snowstorm. Each jingle of the phone announced a new cancellation. Our family had a day to relax—to lounge around a popping fire with *Messiah* chords in the background. I did not have to fight the battle that day.

Read aloud 2 Chronicles 20:1–4.

1. a. What was Jehoshaphat's problem? _____

_____

b. How did he respond to this problem? _____

_____

_____

_____

Read aloud 2 Chronicles 20:5–12.

2. a. Study Jehoshaphat's prayer. What elements of praise do you find? _____

_____

_____

b. What reasons did Jehoshaphat give God for dealing with this problem? _____

_____

_____

   c. Why did he ask for God's judgment? _____

_____

_____

Read aloud 2 Chronicles 20:13–17.

  3. a. Imagine yourself standing in this crowd of people. How would you have felt about Jahaziel's words? Why? _____

_____

_____

_____

    b. What risks would a person take who truly believed this prophecy? _____

_____

_____

Read aloud 2 Chronicles 20:18–30.

  4. In what different ways did the people of Judah worship God? _____

_____

_____

_____

  5. a. What methods did God use to fulfill His prophecy of the previous day? _____

_____

_____

    b. Why do you think God answered Jehoshaphat's prayer in this way? _____

_____

_____

6. Notice the fear of God in surrounding kingdoms (verse 29). In what sense were they correct to say, "The LORD had fought against the enemies of Israel"? _____

_____

Note on verse 29: Here and elsewhere in Chronicles, the writer often refers to Judah as Israel. By this he is not confusing the two kingdoms, but insisting that only the section of the nation that follows God is worthy of the ancient name Israel.

Read 2 Chronicles 20:31–21:3.

7. As you think back over the entire account of Jehoshaphat's life, what did the biblical writers see as his strengths and weaknesses? _____

_____

_____

_____

_____

_____

8. In what different ways did Jehoshaphat demonstrate that he trusted God? _____

_____

_____

_____

9. How did Jehoshaphat balance this trust with responsible effort? _____

_____

_____

_____

10. Look again at the words in 2 Chronicles 20:15–17: "For the battle is not yours. . . . You will not have to fight this battle." When do you most need to hear this kind of message from God? _____

_____

_____

_____

11. What can you learn from Jehoshaphat about the way to pray during such situations? _____

_____

_____

_____

12. God will not fight all of our battles for us. (He didn't fight *all* of Jehoshaphat's. Besides, we might even be in the wrong battle!) But what can you learn from Jehoshaphat's walk with God that will help you cope when you feel battle weary? _____

_____

_____

_____

_____

4

PREPARING FOR STUDY

2 Chronicles 21:4–20;* 1 Kings 22:51–2 Kings 1:18

King Jehoshaphat of Judah and King Ahab of Israel died within a year of each other. Each king had a son who took over his father's throne. Read how each of these new kings (sons of powerful fathers) performed.

Read 2 Chronicles 21:4–20.

1. The end of the account of King Jehoram's life says, "He passed away, to no one's regret, and was buried in the City of David, but not in the tombs of the kings" (verse 20). What did this son of Jehoshaphat do to earn such a eulogy?

2. Was Jehoram more like his father or his father-in-law? How?

3. What penalties did Jehoram and his people pay for his rebellion against God?

Note: In spite of the similarity of names, Joram of Israel is a different person than Jehoram of Judah. Judah's king was a son of Jehoshaphat and Israel's Joram was the brother of Ahaziah (not the one of 21:17) and son of Ahab. The two men were, of course, related by marriage. Jehoram of Judah married Ahab's daughter (2 Chronicles 21:6). There is some

---

*Parallel passage, 2 Kings 8:16–24

problem reconciling the dates when these men were kings. (Compare 2 Kings 1:17 with 3:1.) The discrepancy can probably best be explained by the idea that Jehoram of Judah coreigned for a time with his father.

Read 1 Kings 22:51–2 Kings 1:18.

4. What did Ahaziah do wrong?

5. Why do you think God told Elijah to go up and meet the first messengers of Ahaziah?

6. How was the third captain's request different from the other two?

7. In what sense could these events be viewed as God's protection of His people?

4

ELISHA: PICKING UP THE MANTLE

2 Kings 2

Our family is in a state of transition. Our oldest daughter, Sheri, is graduating from high school and leaving for college. She is a musician. Having studied music since she was nine, she plays all four string instruments—and several instruments of other varieties. Her part-time job during high school has been to teach younger music students. Now she is planning her final student recital. Twenty-one children will perform for the last time as "Sheri's students." Then comes the mad scramble as each student tries to find a capable new teacher.

But number-two daughter is coming up. Lori is a cellist and a flutist. Already the phone is ringing. "Would Lori consider teaching my child? She's just beginning. . . ." It's a scary thought, walking in the footsteps of a respected older sister. Sure, Lori has studied hard and practiced a lot. But she's younger and inexperienced.

The mantle is on the ground. Will she pick it up? Elisha had to make the same decision.

Read aloud 2 Kings 2:1–12.

1. What questions does this story raise in your mind? _____

_____

_____

2. Find on your map the places the two prophets visited. What appears to be the purpose of their trip? _____

_____

Note: Since they went *down* to Bethel (verse 2), the Gilgal mentioned here is probably southwest of Silo, not the one east of Jericho.

3. a. Why do you think Elijah kept telling Elisha to "Stay here"? _____

_____

_____

   b. Why do you think Elisha insisted on staying with Elijah? _____

_____

4. Review, by skimming 1 Kings 19, where Elijah met Elisha. Using the information in that chapter, why might you expect these two prophets to have developed a close relationship in the intervening years? _____

_____

_____

_____

5. a. What did Elisha ask of Elijah? _____

_____

   b. How did Elijah show that this gift was not within his authority to give? _____

_____

6. What do you think Elisha thought and felt when Elijah was taken? _____

_____

_____

7. As you look through these twelve verses again, in what different ways do you see God at work? _____

_____

_____

_____

_____

8. a. Spend a few minutes recalling as many events as you can from Elijah's life. _____

_____

_____

_____

   b. Verse 13 says that Elisha picked up the mantle that had fallen from Elijah. What all do you think this action symbolized? _____

_____

_____

9. If Elisha were immediately to continue the work God had given to Elijah, what challenges would you expect him to face? _____

_____

_____

Read aloud 2 Kings 2:13–25.

10. What benefits can you see from the three-day search, even though the men did not find what they were looking for? _____

_____

_____

11. Three miracles occur in these verses. What effect would each have on Elisha's ministry? _____

_____

_____

12. Young men being mauled by bears, simply because they taunted a prophet, is likely to make us squirm. But if you believed that such an event occurred (and with God's consent), how might this affect your own actions toward people whom God has obviously chosen to do His work? _____

_____

_____

13. In what ways did God provide support for Elisha in the job He had given him to do? (Use the whole chapter.) ___

_____

_____

_____

Note: This was not a job Elisha had taken on purely on his own initiative. First Kings 19:16 shows that God had decreed this work for him.

14. a. Name at least one job that you are reasonably sure God has assigned to you. _____

_____

b. What help has God given you so far in doing that job?

_____

_____

15. a. What obstacles and discouragements are you likely to face in this job? _____

_____

_____

_____

b. How might your past experiences of God's support help you through future obstacles? _____

_____

_____

_____

5

PREPARING FOR STUDY

2 Kings 4:1–6:23

1. Make a chart showing each of Elisha's miracles recorded here.

	What does this story help you know about the times of Elisha?	Who was helped?	What power was demonstrated?
4:1–7			
4:8–17			
4:18–37			
4:38–41			
4:42–44			
5:1–19			
5:20–27			
6:1–7			
6:8–23			

2. What do these events say about how God uses His power?

5

ELISHA: FAITH IN HARD TIMES

2 Kings 6:24—7:20

I have a friend who has been plagued by seeming disasters: One daughter joined a cult; another daughter couldn't seem to stay married—to anyone; a son died of cancer; her husband requires frequent psychiatric care.

What has she done wrong? Nothing really. She has done a better-than-average job of parenting and she possesses a more-than-normal dose of stability. Through all the trauma, she has maintained an uncomplicated trust in God. And occasionally we see a glimmer of purpose around her string of disasters. This larger view shows all of us close to her that her trust is justified.

Read aloud 2 Kings 6:24—7:2.

1. What indications do you see that the situation in Samaria was desperate? _____

_____

_____

_____

_____

Note: Samaria was part of the northern kingdom, Israel. (See map, page 19.)

2. a. Review 1 Kings 20:42–43, where Ahab had thoroughly defeated Ben-Hadad (twice) but spared the king's life when he begged for mercy. Try to recall your feelings when you first read about God's condemnation of Ahab. _____

_____

b. How do these feelings change in view of the events described in 2 Kings 6? _____

_____

_____

3. Read Leviticus 26:14–15 and 27–29 to discover some of the terms of the ancient covenant God had made with His people. With these terms as a part of their history, what areas might the people begin to examine in order to find a cause for the siege? _____

_____

4. Notice each reference to God in 2 Kings 6:24–7:2. What does each speaker seem to believe about God's relationship to the siege? _____

_____

_____

_____

Read aloud 2 Kings 7:3–16.

5. Why did the four lepers go to the Aramean camp? _____

_____

6. What explanation does the writer of Kings offer for the end of the siege? _____

_____

_____

_____

7. If you had been one of those lepers, what would you have done when you discovered the Aramean camp deserted? _____

_____

8. a. What cautions did the king exercise when he heard the news of an empty enemy camp? _____

_____

_____

_____

   b. What do these actions reveal concerning the emotional state of the people at that time? _____

_____

_____

Read aloud 2 Kings 7:17–20.

9. Why do you think the king's officer died? _____

_____

_____

10. People often think that God's arena encompasses times of peace and love and tranquility. How does this passage enlarge that view of God? _____

_____

_____

_____

11. Why is it hard to trust God during hard times? _____

_____

_____

_____

12. a. What is the biggest disaster you have had to face since you began to trust God? _____

_____

_____

b. What did that period in your life teach you about God?

_____

_____

13. What can you do during times of relative calm that would prepare you to trust God when times are hard? ___

_____

_____

6

PREPARING FOR STUDY

2 Kings 8

1. What are some ways that God continued to take care of the Shunammite woman (verses 1–6)?

2. Why did Elisha weep (verses 7–15)?

3. In what ways was Jehoram's reign a step backward for his country, Judah (verses 16–24)?

4. a. What explanations can you offer for the close relationship between Israel and Judah during Ahaziah's reign (verses 25–29)?

   b. Do you see this link between the two nations as working for or against spiritual health for the people? Why?

5. If God were determined to protect the spiritual well-being of His people, what would you expect Him to do?

6

JEHU: GOD'S AVENGER

2 Kings 9–10*

God's Executioner

Fly, killer Jehu
Riding your chariot
A madman across the plains

"He drives like Jehu!"
Swallows my messengers
And spits them out his tail

Tremble Ahab in your grave
You spilt your seed on the ground
One-hundred-fold
And Jehu rides to lick it up

---

*Parallel passage, 2 Chronicles 22:1–9

Read aloud all of 2 Kings 9 and 10.

1. What disturbs you most about this account? _____

_____

_____

_____

2. a. What did God tell Jehu to do? _____

_____

b. What special instructions did Elisha give his messenger? _____

_____

_____

c. What reasons can you think of for these instructions?

_____

_____

3. Review the history leading up to these events:

a. First Kings 15:28–30 and 16:9–12. What happened to the families of Jeroboam and Baasha (earlier kings of Israel)? How, and why? _____

_____

_____

b. First Kings 18:4 and 19:10. Why is the word *avenge* in 2 Kings 9:7 appropriate for what God intended to do?

_____

c. First Kings 19:16–17. As you think back over events that led to these words from God, why would Elijah have felt great relief at hearing them? _____

_____

_____

    d. First Kings 21:17–29. What reasons do you find here
       for Jehu's actions? _____

_____

_____

_____

4. Return to 2 Kings 9 and 10. Where were the major
   characters of this account when the story opened? (Use
   your map.) Why was each person where he or she was?

_____

_____

_____

5. Make a list of all the people Jehu killed. _____

_____

_____

_____

_____

6. a. Using your list from question 5, outline Jehu's strategy
     for securing his own position as king. _____

_____

_____

_____

   b. What ideas in his strategy seem particularly cunning to
     you? _____

_____

_____

_____

7. What evidence do you see that Jehu killed the leaders of Baal worship not simply because of his desire to worship the true God? _____

_____

_____

_____

8. Would you classify Jehu as a good or an evil king? _____

_____

Why? _____

_____

_____

_____

9. Why do you think God allowed this slaughter by Jehu?

_____

_____

10. If God is good and God is sovereign, why do we see wholesale violence in our world? _____

_____

_____

_____

_____

_____

7

PREPARING FOR STUDY

2 Chronicles 22:10–12

1. Straighten out the relationships between the people mentioned in these two chapters.

   a. Who was Athaliah?

   How was she related to King Ahaziah?

   to Joash?

   to Jezebel and Ahab? (See 2 Kings 8:16–18, 25–27.)

   b. Who was Joash?

   How was he related to King Ahaziah?

   to Athaliah?

   to King Jehoram? (See 2 Chronicles 22:1.)

   to Jehosheba?

   c. Who was Jehosheba?

   How was she related to King Jehoram?

   to King Ahaziah?

   to Joash?

   to Jehoiada?

2. Why would Athaliah want to kill the child Joash? (See also 2 Chronicles 21:4 and 22:1.)

3. Why would the temple of God be a likely place to hide from Queen Athaliah?

4. When has God's house (or His people) been a refuge to you? Thank Him for this.

7

JOASH: PROTÉGÉ TO A PRIEST

*2 Chronicles 23–24**

A car loaded with household goods stands waiting in the driveway. I hug my spiritual mentor, my best friend, good-by. I close the car door behind her and watch her drive away while a gnawing emptiness digs at my gut.

My mind goes back over our intense times of searching the Scriptures together, comfortable walks in the woods, shouting rides on a snow sled, tearful problem-solving, brief honest prayers for one another. And I know I can never relive those times. They are gone, with her, to the West Coast.

It hasn't happened—yet. But the scene has crossed my mind often enough for me to ask myself some hard questions: Where is my faith anchored? In her or in God? If she goes, where will I turn for spiritual nurture? Am I a grown woman, able to find constructive ways to meet my own needs? Or am

*Parallel passage, 2 Kings 11–12

60

I still wandering, umbilical cord in hand, looking for a place to plug it in?

Read aloud 2 Chronicles 23:1–11.

1. What groundwork did Jehoiada lay to ensure that the child Joash would safely become king? _____

_____

_____

_____

_____

_____

2. Why would the covenant be of value to Joash? _____

_____

Read aloud 2 Chronicles 23:12–24:3.

3. Notice the dramatic moment described in verses 12–13. How would you have felt if you had stood in that crowd?

_____

_____

4. Why do you think Jehoiada said, "Do not put her to death at the temple of the LORD"? _____

_____

_____

5. What steps did Jehoiada take to establish spiritual change in Judah? _____

_____

_____

_____

6. Notice the pageantry of verses 20–21. What would the movements of Joash symbolize to the people? _____

_____

_____

7. How would you describe the relationship between Jehoiada and Joash? _____

_____

_____

_____

Read aloud 2 Chronicles 24:4–16.

8. a. What problem did Joash have in getting money to restore the temple? _____

_____

b. How did he resolve that problem? _____

_____

_____

_____

_____

9. What indications do you see that Joash tried to make restoring the temple an honest process? _____

_____

_____

_____

_____

10. Think back over Jehoiada's life. Of what value was he to the people of Judah? _____

_____

_____

_____

_____

Read aloud 2 Chronicles 24:17–27.

11. What changes came to Judah after Jehoiada's death? ____

_____

_____

_____

_____

12. Why was it hard to be a prophet in the later part of Joash's reign? _____

_____

_____

_____

13. Why would you not expect Joash to take this kind of turn? _____

_____

_____

_____

14. a. What person is most responsible for your own spiritual development? _____

b. How has that person helped you? _____

_____

_____

_____

c. What could you be doing that would help you to continue to mature spiritually if that person were removed from your life? _____

_____

_____

_____

_____

15. a. Think of one person for whom you are a spiritual guardian. _____

b. How can you help that person be ready to continue spiritual growth even if you were no longer available to help? _____

_____

_____

_____

8

PREPARING FOR STUDY

1. Divide your past into several periods of history. For example: grade school, high school, college, career; or, childhood, early adulthood, late adulthood.

2. Write down a major loss you sustained during each time. It might be a person, a thing, an opportunity, an ideal.

3. Now write something that God allowed you to learn because of that loss.

4. How have you built on the lessons you learned then?

8

HAZAEL: AN ENEMY TO MAKE PROPHETS WEEP

2 Kings 13

My friend Jan sat at her kitchen table and cried. Several months ago her husband had lost his job. Their living room now stood warehouse-vacant; the furniture had been repossessed. The large country home in which they lived was next in line; the bank would no longer carry the loan. And now (surprise) a new baby was on the way. Jan would also have to give up her job.

Losses like these make us take a hard look at ourselves. Have we displeased God? Have we made foolish errors in planning? Or are we simply caught in the fallout of a world that is overrun by sin?

Sometimes we can find no answers, but if we bring the questions to God, we are likely to come away with something of value to sustain us through that time. And God may even use those losses to teach us something about Himself.

Israel suffered staggering losses to Hazael. But God did not abandon His people. In fact, God was trying hard to get their attention.

Read aloud 2 Kings 13:1–13.

1. Describe the conditions in Israel during the reign of Jehoahaz and Jehoash. _____

   _____

   _____

   _____

   _____

   _____

Note: In some translations Jehoash is called Joash. But he is not the same person as the king of Judah.

2. What connection do you see between Israel's response to God and her political situation? _____

   _____

   _____

   _____

Read aloud 2 Kings 13:14–21.

3. What do you think King Jehoash meant when he said to Elisha, "My father! My father! The chariots and horsemen of Israel!"? _____

   _____

   _____

   _____

4. a. Why do you think Elisha had Jehoash act out his message from God? _____

_____

b. What meaning did Elisha ascribe to the drama? _____

_____

_____

5. Think back over the events you remember from Elisha's life. What do you think God intended Israel to know about Himself through this prophet? _____

_____

_____

_____

_____

6. What effect was Elisha's final miracle likely to have on the Israelites who saw it? _____

_____

_____

Read again Elisha's encounter with Hazael in 2 Kings 8:7–15.

7. a. What contrasts do you see between the surface gestures of their meeting and their underlying meaning?

_____

_____

_____

_____

b. Why did Elisha go to Damascus? (See also 1 Kings 19:15.) _____

_____

8. a. Why did Elisha weep? _____

_____

_____

_____

b. What does this story reveal of Hazael's character? ____

_____

_____

Read aloud the following additional accounts of Hazael (use your chart and map to follow the flow of events):

9. What did Israel or Judah give up in each of these encounters?

2 Kings 9:14–15 _____

_____

2 Kings 10:32 _____

_____

2 Chronicles 24:23–25 _____

_____

2 Kings 12:17–18 _____

_____

2 Kings 13:3 _____

_____

2 Kings 13:7 _____

_____

Note: According to Assyrian records, Ahab's army (40 years earlier) had 2,000 chariots and 10,000 footmen (*New Bible Commentary*, p. 357).

10. By the time Hazael died, what territory and power was left to Israel? _____

_____

_____

_____

11. What do you think God wanted His people to learn through these losses to Hazael? (Support your answers from the passages surrounding Hazael's life.) _____

_____

_____

_____

Read aloud 2 Kings 13:22–25.

12. Why did God bring relief from Hazael's attacks? _____

_____

13. When have you seen evidence of God's mercy in a time of personal loss? _____

_____

_____

14. How has personal loss increased your trust in God? _____

_____

_____

9

PREPARING FOR STUDY

2 Chronicles 25–27* 2 Kings 14:23–29; 15:8–31; Hosea

Read 2 Chronicles 25–27 and 2 Kings 14:23–29 and 15:8–31.

1. Chart the kings recorded for this time period (see pp. 20–21).

2. Scan the chapters for references to God or the Lord. What do you see as God's role in this period of Jewish history?

3. a. God sent Hosea to prophesy during the reign of Jeroboam II. Read some of his work in Hosea 1–3. If Gomer represents the Jewish people and Hosea symbolizes God, what does the story of their marriage say has gone wrong?

   b. What does this marriage story suggest will happen in the future of Israel and Judah?

4. a. Read Hosea 14. (If you're ambitious, read the intervening chapters too.) Considering what you have read of the history of this era (Kings and Chronicles passages), what does this chapter say the people should do?

   b. What hope does it offer?

---

*Parallel passages, 2 Kings 14:1–22; 15:1–7, 33–38

	King's name	Israel or Judah?	Number of years ruled	Good or evil?	How did he die?	Accomplish-ments
1.						
2.						
3.						
4.						
5.						
6.						
7.						
8.						
9.						

9

ISAIAH: PROPHET OF VISION

Isaiah 6

John Bright in his *History of Israel* says,

> In all of her history, Israel produced few figures of greater
> stature than Isaiah. Called to the prophetic office (Isa.
> 6:1) in the year of Uzziah's death (742), for fifty years he
> towered over the contemporary scene, and though
> perhaps few in his day realized it, more than any other
> individual, guided the nation through her hour of tragedy
> and crisis. (p. 290)

Isaiah, inspired by God, composed one of the most
powerful books of the Old Testament; yet he lived and
worked in a period of national chaos. Today you will discuss
Isaiah's personal encounter with the Holy God.

Read aloud Isaiah 6:1–4.

1. a. Suppose you had stood in Isaiah's shoes during the
events of verses 1–4. What would your five senses

have revealed to you? _____

_____

_____

_____

_____

b. What qualities of God does this picture suggest? _____

_____

_____

2. Close your eyes for a moment and try to imagine the scene described by these verses. What would be your inner response to this experience? _____

_____

_____

Read aloud Isaiah 6:5—8.

3. What different responses do you find here? _____

_____

_____

_____

4. Why do you think Isaiah used the word "unclean"? _____

_____

_____

5. Why was the live coal an appropriate response to Isaiah's feelings of verse 5? _____

_____

_____

_____

_____

_____

6. a. How did the previous events of the chapter prepare Isaiah to say in verse 8, "Here am I. Send me!"? _____

_____

_____

b. In view of these preceding events, what risks was Isaiah accepting when he said this to God? _____

_____

_____

7. a. Are you able to say "Here am I. Send me!" to God? Why, or why not? _____

_____

_____

b. What should a modern-day believer consider before making this kind of commitment to God? _____

_____

_____

_____

Read aloud Isaiah 6:9–13.

8. What was going to be hard about Isaiah's job? _____

_____

_____

_____

9. Finish this sentence about the future of Judah in as many ways as you can: It will be so bad in Judah that . . . _____

_____

_____

_____

_____

10. If God knew that His people would reject the appeal to return to Him, why do you think He sent Isaiah to them?

_____

_____

_____

11. a. Notice the phrase "holy seed" of verse 13. Why does this phrase raise hope in the context Isaiah has just described? _____

_____

_____

b. The "holy seed" is further defined by the next chapter and by a New Testament quotation of the promise. Read aloud Isaiah 7:14 and Matthew 1:18–25. How do these passages amplify the hope Isaiah raised by his term "holy seed"? _____

_____

_____

_____

_____

12. What contrasts do you see between Isaiah's experience of "God with us" in Isaiah 6:1–4 and the "God with us" of Matthew 1? _____

_____

_____

_____

13. How can you integrate both of these true pictures of God? _____

_____

_____

_____

14. Meditate for a moment on the phrase, "Immanuel: God with us."

a. What does this phrase mean to you? _____

_____

_____

_____

b. How can you respond to it on a day-to-day basis? ___

_____

_____

10

PREPARING FOR STUDY

Micah

Read all of Micah sometime during this week.

1. a. What actions of the people had earned God's wrath?

   b. What actions of the leaders?

   c. What actions of the false prophets?

2. What accusations show that the people did not see the gravity of their situation?

3. What did Micah predict would happen to Judah?

4. What contrasts do you find between Micah's description of the last days (4:1–8) and the way Judah had chosen to live now?

5. What doom and what hope come out of Micah's references to a "remnant" (2:12; 4:7; 5:7–8; 7:18)?

6. Compare Micah 5:2–5 with Matthew 2:1–6 and John 10:14–18. What further hope does Micah's promise offer a doomed nation?

7. Read Micah 7:7–9. If you were living under evil King Ahaz, how would these verses help you cope?

8. Read again Micah 7:18–20. How does Micah's faith grow out of the nature of God?

9. Meditate on the words of Micah 6:8.

10. How can you follow these three standards this week?

10

AHAZ: FAITHLESS IN TROUBLE

2 Kings 16*

Eleven years ago I suffered a miscarriage. We had two girls, but we had planned two more children—boys, we hoped. Already I had lost one baby in the first trimester. Now I prayed my way through those first three months again. But warning flags arose, and the pregnancy was in trouble. Shortly into the second trimester, the baby was gone.

And I was mad! I had done all the right things. I had been especially careful about diet, medicines, activities. I had prayed constantly. But the baby had died inside me anyway. I prayed one angry prayer to God and then stopped praying altogether—for a while.

But God is merciful. He gave us two boys (adopted). Later I had to ask, "Why was I so mad? Is God only God for the

*Parallel passages, 2 Chronicles 28; Isaiah 7–8; 14:28–32

good times? Is He a handy tool for me to get what I want and to lay aside when He (in my view) doesn't deliver?"

My response to trouble was not so different from King Ahaz's. When the going got tough, Ahaz switched sides.

Read aloud 2 Kings 16:1–6.

1. In what different ways did Ahaz express his idolatry? ____

_____

_____

2. What military crisis did Ahaz face? (Use your chart and map to picture this.) _____

_____

_____

_____

Read aloud an expanded account of these events in Isaiah 7:1–12.

3. Why might God's description of the enemies of Ahaz have given him courage to fight against them? _____

_____

_____

_____

4. How does the setting of Isaiah's meeting with Ahaz add urgency to their conversation? _____

_____

_____

5. a. What did Isaiah predict? _____

_____

b. What did God invite Ahaz to do? _____

_____

_____

c. How did Ahaz respond? _____

_____

Read aloud 2 Kings 16:7–19.

6. In view of the message Ahaz had received from God, why do you think he appealed to Assyria? _____

_____

_____

_____

_____

7. What did help from Assyria cost the people of Judah? ___

_____

_____

_____

8. What reasons did Ahaz have to be wary of this alliance?

_____

_____

9. What specific changes did Ahaz make in the temple? ___

_____

_____

_____

_____

_____

10. Look up God's statement about arrangements in His tabernacle (Exodus 26:30) and David's statement about plans for arranging the temple (1 Chronicles 28:19). In view of these, what was Ahaz saying by his actions in the temple? _____

_____

_____

_____

11. Read 2 Chronicles 28:22–23 for an evaluation of the life of Ahaz. What errors do you see in Ahaz's reasoning?

_____

_____

_____

12. a. Bring to mind a situation that spells trouble to you. (Samples: Your church has a major fight; someone you have prayed for dies; your husband loses his job; your parents announce a divorce.) _____

_____

b. Take an honest look at your behavior patterns, and jot some notes about the way you think you would react to the troublesome situation you have in mind. _____

_____

_____

_____

13. a. In what ways does your response to trouble seem to be a search for other gods and other altars? _____

_____

_____

b. To what extent does your response to trouble reflect a determined faith in God? _____

_____

_____

_____

14. Much of our worship can become, like Ahaz's, an attempt to get what we want out of God. When this occurs, we need to ask ourselves, "Who is my god: God or me?" How can you make your worship less self-centered and more God-centered? _____

_____

_____

_____

_____

11

PREPARING FOR STUDY

Amos 1:1–5:3

God gave Amos, a shepherd from Judah, the difficult task of traveling north to Israel and prophesying against this rival sister nation. It was the era of Jeroboam II, a period of political and economic prosperity. But Amos, like other prophets, saw the future. He warned the people that this interlude of high living would be short-lived.

Read Amos 1:1–5:3. (Ambitious? Read the whole book. You'll be rewarded by an exhilarating picture near the end of an even more distant future.)

1. Focus on Amos 1:1–2:5.

    a. Find on your map each nation against which Amos prophesied.

    b. What crimes and judgments are listed?

    c. How do you think a listener in Israel would feel at the end of these pronouncements?

2. Focus on Amos 2:6–16.

    a. What did God accuse Israel of doing?

    b. What had He done for Israel in the past?

    c. What did He say He would do now?

3. Focus on Amos 3.

a. How does the writer use cause and effect to illustrate the validity of his prophetic message?

b. What is that message?

4. Focus on Amos 4:1–5:3.

a. How had Israel misinterpreted and misused its current wealth?

b. What evidences of God's persistent love does Amos detail?

c. How does the final section of this passage help define Amos's words, "Prepare to meet your God, O Israel"?

5. What dangers to spiritual health do you find in your own prosperity? Talk to God about these.

11

HOSHEA: IDOLATRY'S REWARD

2 Kings 17

We had just bought a new house, a three-bedroom ranch on an acre of land. I could plant fruit trees and a vegetable garden. Our children could run and yell without disturbing neighbors. Our kitchen was big enough for two people to work together, and all six of us could sit down at the table. Best of all, there were windows everywhere. (I love being able to feel like I'm halfway outside while enjoying the cushy comfort of a living room sofa.)

My brother visited us then and asked matter-of-factly, "Is this house your goal in life?" He meant, "Do you plan to stay here, or are you planning to 'move up'?"

I knew what he *meant*, but I chose to answer what he actually asked. "No, of course not," I said stoutly. "I don't think *any* house could be my goal in life."

I could answer with confidence because I'm just not a house person, as my grubby kitchen floor and cluttered linen closet will testify. But had Dan chosen another topic (such as work, friends, family, church), I might have had to squirm a little. Idolatry is insidious for us all.

Read aloud 2 Kings 17.

1. How does this chapter make you feel? _____

_____

_____

2. Notice the people and places in verses 1–6. How do these verses outline the final steps to Israel's death as a nation? _____

_____

_____

3. Why was the Assyrian technique of conquering an effective way to wipe out a nation? _____

_____

_____

Note: In all of history, we never again see this nation, Israel. In fact, they are often called "the ten lost tribes."

4. a Review the list of sins (there are about twenty) in verses 7–22. What common characteristics do you find? _____

_____

_____

b. Try to summarize Israel's sin in one sentence? _____

_____

_____

5. Twice the writer of Kings says of Israel, "The LORD removed them from his presence." What did it mean to Israel to be removed from the presence of God? _____

_____

_____

_____

6. Notice the references to Judah, Israel's sister nation to the south. If you had been living in Judah at the time of the events recorded here, what might you have learned about the relationship of God to His chosen people? ____

_____

_____

_____

7. Use your chart to review the history of the northern kingdom. What turning points led to its death? _____

_____

_____

_____

_____

_____

8. When the prophet Amos prophesied against Israel, he said repeatedly, "Yet you would not return to Me." As you think over Israel's history, in what different ways would you begin that statement? _____

_____

_____

_____

_____

_____ and yet you would not return to Me.

9. Look again at the events recorded in 2 Kings 17:24–41. How do these verses help explain the friction between Jews and Samaritans in New Testament times? _____

_____

_____

_____

10. Review God's commands to His people before they entered this land: Exodus 34:10–16.

   a. Why did Israel find it hard to serve one God alone? ___

   _____

   _____

   _____

   b. Why did the new Samaritans? _____

   _____

   _____

   _____

   c. Why do we? _____

   _____

   _____

   _____

11. The people of Israel, and later, the Samaritans, tried to worship the true God at the same time they served other gods. Why didn't this work? _____

_____

_____

12. Take a few moments to jot honest answers to these questions. (No need to share them with the group.)

I couldn't live without _____

_____

When my mind is idle, it automatically turns to _____

_____

If I could have anything in the world, I would choose ____

_____

The most important thing (person) in the world to me is

_____

I know God wants me to _____ but I can't.

13. In what areas of your life do you need to be alert to the temptation of idolatry? _____

_____

_____

_____

14. How might your study of Israel help you worship only God? _____

_____

_____

_____

12

PREPARING FOR STUDY

2 Chronicles 29–31

Read 2 Chronicles 29:1–19.

1. What explanations did Hezekiah make for the hardships that faced his nation?

2. What steps did the priests and Levites take, under Hezekiah's direction, to purify the temple?

Read 2 Chronicles 29:20–36.

3. How did the people express worship to God?

4. What elements of joy accompanied this worship?

Read 2 Chronicles 30:1–31:1.

5. How was spiritual cleansing brought to Jerusalem?

6. Find as many expressions of joy as you can in this chapter. How might you make your own worship more joyful?

Read 2 Chronicles 31.

7. How did Hezekiah insure continued orderly worship?

8. Review 2 Chronicles 30:20, 27; 31:20–21. In view of these, what would you expect from God during the reign of Hezekiah?

12

HEZEKIAH: KING IN CRISIS

Isaiah 36–37*

Taunts—with two sons less than a year apart, I've heard my share of them. Two boys crouch over small toy cars that zoom down newly created roads in the dirt. But this peaceful scene is too often interrupted by, "Hey! quit muckin' up my road!"

"It's not your road. I made it."

"Well, my car's on it; so it's my road."

"Hey, that's not your car; it's mine. See—mine had the wobbly front wheel."

"My wheel got wobbly too. Hey, get your knee out of the road; you're wreckin' it. Da-ad!"

"Dad's not gonna do anything. I'll tell him you took my car. Da-ad!"

Small children—each convinced that dad will take his

---

*Parallel passages, 2 Kings 18–19; 2 Chronicles 32:9–23

side. Small issues—hardly worth the mental energy it takes
to pocket the cars and tell the boys to fight over something
else for a while.

But when nations play such taunting games, thousands of
lives are at stake. And if one king is correct when he says to
another, "Your God's not going to help you; He's on my
side," a whole nation may disappear as quickly as a finger-
width dirt road beneath a careless knee.

Read aloud Isaiah 36.

1. Notice the people and places in verses 1–4. How do
   they help you define what was about to happen? _____

   _____

   _____

   _____

   _____

2. What reasons did Hezekiah have to take this meeting
   seriously? (See also 2 Kings 18:13–16.) _____

   _____

   _____

   _____

   _____

Note: "Excavations at Lachish, which Sennacherib stormed,
reveal, along with evidences of destruction, a huge pit into
which the remains of some 1,500 bodies had been dumped
and covered with pig bones and other debris—presumably
the garbage of the Assyrian army" (Bright, p. 286).

3. In what ways did the Assyrian field commander misuse
   truth to undermine Hezekiah's people? _____

_____

_____

_____

_____

_____

_____

4. If you had been on the wall listening to this conversation, what would you have worried about? _____

_____

_____

_____

Read aloud Isaiah 37:1–8.

5. What words and phrases show that Hezekiah took the Assyrian threat seriously? _____

_____

_____

_____

_____

6. a. In what sense was this a spiritual as well as a political confrontation? _____

_____

_____

_____

b. Would the spiritual dimension bring comfort or fear to Hezekiah? Why? _____

_____

_____

_____

Read aloud Isaiah 37:9–20.

7. What spiritual threat did potential help from Egypt bring to Hezekiah? _____

_____

_____

8. How was Hezekiah's response to the Assyrian letter rooted in the character of God? (Notice both words and actions.) _____

_____

_____

_____

_____

Read aloud Isaiah 37:21–35.

9. Divide Isaiah's song into 8 or 9 stanzas. Title each with a quality of God. _____

_____

_____

_____

_____

_____

10. This message from Isaiah is often called a "taunt song." In what ways did it rebut the Assyrian taunts that Hezekiah had endured? _____

_____

_____

_____

_____

_____

Read aloud Isaiah 37:36—38.

11. What do these final events contribute to this story's revelations about God? _____

_____

_____

12. In what ways is Hezekiah a good model for handling crises? _____

_____

_____

_____

13. If you were to write out your own personal crisis and spread it, in prayer, before God, how would it affect your praying? _____

_____

_____

_____

13

PREPARING FOR STUDY

*Isaiah 38**

Read Isaiah 38:1–8.

1. What evidences do you see that God was intimately concerned with Hezekiah's life?

2. Why do you think God first told Hezekiah to "put your house in order"?

3. Would you rather die unexpectedly or know that you would die in exactly fifteen years? Why?

Read Isaiah 38:9–22.

4. What does Hezekiah's poem reveal of his view of death?

5. How did Hezekiah believe his life would be changed as a result of his illness and reprieve?

6. How would you expect this experience to affect his family relationships? (See especially verse 19.)

7. Meditate on the three parts of verse 17. Name a situation in your own life that each section describes. Praise God for His work in each of these events.

*Parallel passages, 2 Kings 20:1–11; 2 Chronicles 32:24–26

13

MANASSEH: ONE GIANT STEP BACKWARD

2 Kings 20–21*

Our friends Bob and Dottie and their children are missionaries to a primitive tribe of Indians in South America. They've spent, off and on, fifteen years there. After some initial awkwardness, they were well received. They donned the long white tunics of the tribal people, carried their woven handbags, and wore tiny beaded necklaces. They washed clothing native-style by beating it on the riverside rocks. They carried their babies like papooses. (It was easier for climbing mountains.) They ate native food—the local parasites had a heyday.

And the Indians took them in—it seemed. They helped Bob and Dottie learn the language. They came for medical help when they were sick or wounded. They leafed through the reading-readiness books, all the while jabbering, "Make

*Parallel passages, Isaiah 39; 2 Chronicles 32:24–33:25

the book talk.'' God seemed ready to use them to help bring these people into His kingdom.

Then drug traffic swept the area. Speculators bought the land or simply massacred Indians reluctant to sell. Twentieth-century viruses decimated the tribe. Bad health and accidents plagued their own family. Bob and his young son were falsely arrested and jailed. The area had become too dangerous for mission work. In fact, only two-thirds of the Indians remained alive. And some who were left looked at them with hostile eyes.

Can we still trust God when all the trends point counter to what we know of His purposes? One of the advantages of studying the Old Testament is seeing, in a few pages, God moving through hundreds of years of history. It may help us trust God's unseen purposes for our own small page.

Read aloud 2 Kings 20:1–11.

1. What do the details in the communication between God and Hezekiah reveal about their relationship? _____

_____

_____

_____

Read aloud 2 Kings 20:12–21.

2. Why do you think Hezekiah treated the messengers from Babylon the way he did? _____

_____

_____

_____

Note: This is the first biblical reference to Babylon except in 2 Kings 17 where its people are captives of Assyria.

3. What connections did Isaiah find between Hezekiah's actions and the future of Judah? _____

_____

_____

_____

4. a. How would you expect Hezekiah to respond to Isaiah's prophecy? _____

_____

_____

   b. What explanation can you offer for the response recorded here? _____

_____

_____

Read aloud 2 Kings 21:1–18.

5. When you try to imagine life in Judah under Manasseh's reign, what pictures come to your mind? _____

_____

_____

_____

6. Find as many references to the people of Judah as you can in verses 7–15. How do these help explain why Manasseh was able to make such a total reversal of his father's reforms? _____

_____

_____

_____

_____

7. How does the prophet's use of symbols help illustrate the future? _____

_____

_____

_____

_____

_____

8. Suppose you were living in Judah at this time. You heard this prophecy and believed it to be true. What would you do? _____

_____

_____

_____

9. Why do you think no Old Testament prophet claims to have written during Manasseh's reign? _____

_____

_____

Read aloud 2 Kings 21:19–26.

10. In what ways did Amon's reign seem to appropriately follow Manasseh's actions? _____

_____

_____

_____

11. Look back at Hezekiah's situation in 2 Kings 20:1–11. If Hezekiah could have known the future, do you think he would have wanted God to add fifteen years to his life? Why, or why not? _____

_____

_____

12. Manasseh is described as "the most evil of all the kings." Why do you think God let him rule fifty-five years, longer than any other king? _____

_____

_____

13. What do you know of God that would enable you to trust Him in the face of popular trends against what you know is right? _____

_____

_____

_____

_____

14. Think of some anti-God trends that now touch your life. How can you serve God in your response to these trends? _____

_____

_____

_____

_____

14

PREPARING FOR STUDY

Nahum 1; Zephaniah 1; Jeremiah 1–2

Three prophets wrote during the reign of Josiah. Prepare for this week's discussion by sampling each of their works. If you want to cover all of the known prophetic writings of the era, read Nahum 1–3, Zephaniah 1–3, and Jeremiah 1–6.

Read Nahum 1.

1. What qualities of God described here inspire you to worship Him?

2. What relief did Nahum promise Judah from Nineveh, the capital city of Assyria?

Read Zephaniah 1.

3. Why should Judah have not felt overly relieved to know that God promised to punish Assyria?

4. What prophecy do you find here that has probably not yet been fulfilled, even today?

Read Jeremiah 1–2.

5. What literary beauty do you find in this passage?

6. In what ways did Jeremiah's call to prophesy prepare him for a difficult job?

7. How does God use the symbol of a sexually promiscuous woman to describe His relationship with Judah?

8. If you had been living under the ministry of these prophets, what would you have expected in Judah's future? How would you have prepared for this?

14

JOSIAH: BOY KING; ADULT REFORMER

2 Kings 22:1–23:30*

Seniors in high school get a little huffy about restrictive school rules such as hall passes and washroom permits. Even teachers are not immune. When my daughter's music teacher, accustomed to working with diligent honors students, was confronted with the request for one more hall pass for an in-building errand, he wrote, "Sheri has my permission to be in the hall so that she can check the drug supply in her locker. Antonia is her bodyguard." (They weren't stopped.)

There's something inside us that grates against laws—of any kind—unless, of course, we've had to live a long time without them. Judah had such an experience.

*Parallel passage, 2 Chronicles 34–35

Read aloud 2 Kings 22:1–23:3.

1. What steps led to finding the Book of the Law? _____

   _____

   _____

2. In view of the reactions to the Book of the Law, what can you guess of its content? _____

   _____

   _____

   _____

3. a. What can you know about Huldah? _____

   _____

   _____

   b. Look again at God's word through Huldah. What could Josiah know about God from her message? _____

   _____

   _____

   _____

   _____

4. Notice the scene described in 2 Kings 23:1–3. What effect would you expect this to have on the people? _____

   _____

   _____

Read aloud 2 Kings 23:4–30.

5. Look for details in the sixteen reforms that Josiah instituted. In view of these, what would it have been like to live and worship in Judah just prior to Josiah's reign?

_____

_____

_____

_____

_____

6. How would you expect the life of an ordinary lay person to be affected by these changes? _____

_____

_____

_____

_____

7. Look again at verse 25. As you think over the record of Josiah's life, what specific acts does this summary statement reflect? _____

_____

_____

_____

_____

8. a. Notice particularly the following words and phrases: "turned to the LORD," "heart," "soul," "strength," "all the Law." If someone were to evaluate these areas at the end of your life, which of them would likely be weak? _____

_____

b. How can you begin now to shore up that weak area?

_____

_____

_____

_____

9. Taking into consideration the prophecies in these two chapters, the prophets of the era, and Josiah's reforms, would you be optimistic or pessimistic about Judah's future? _____

_____

_____

_____

Read 2 Chronicles 35:20–27.

10. Would you say that Josiah died an honorable death? Why, or why not? _____

_____

_____

_____

11. In what different ways did Josiah show respect for the Law of God? (Draw from all of 2 Kings 22–23.) _____

_____

_____

_____

Note: For the purpose of these questions define God's law as "God's standards of behavior for His people, as recorded in Scripture."

12. In what ways do you fall short of the response Josiah gave to God's law? _____

_____

_____

_____

13. What relationship do you see between our response to God's law and our concept of God? _____

_____

_____

_____

_____

14. What steps could you take to bring your response to God's law into line with what you believe to be true of God? _____

_____

_____

_____

_____

15

PREPARING FOR STUDY

Jeremiah 36; Ezekiel 8; Habakkuk 1—3

Three prophets are known to have prophesied to Judah during this era of history. Jeremiah and Ezekiel are major prophets (they wrote long books), so we will sample only one chapter of each as we prepare for study. Habakkuk is a minor prophet (short book), so we'll read all of his jewel-like example of prophetic literature.

Read Jeremiah 36.

1. Why was the scroll important?

2. What does the official reaction to Jeremiah's scroll tell you about the spiritual climate in Judah?

3. What do Jehoiakim's actions of verse 23 suggest about his attitude toward any unpleasant words from God?

Read Ezekiel 8.

4. What pictures does Ezekiel draw to show the condition of Judah's religious leaders?

5. What emotions might a godly man like Ezekiel feel after seeing all this?

Read Habakkuk 1—3.

6. What is the gist of Habakkuk's complaint?

7. Why were the Babylonians not the kind of answer Habakkuk had hoped to receive from God?

8. How did Habakkuk draw on his faith in the face of this message?

9. Meditate on Habakkuk 3:17–19. How might this song help you through a siege of personal loss?

15

ZEDEKIAH: END OF THE LINE

2 Kings 23:31–25:21*

Ezekiel 8

Dig you prophet, Dig in the wall
Probe the hole that opens to the night
Weep Ezekiel, Weep for your call

Crumble small the whitewash with your awl
Daubed by holy priests who smothered light
Dig you prophet, Dig in the wall

Dig you deeper, Dig back to the fall
Hasten shepherd, see your flocks in flight
Weep Ezekiel, Weep for your call

Hide your eyes and shrink from the small
Door that dries your bones as if you might
Not dig. You watchman, Dig in the wall

*Parallel passages, Jeremiah 7–52; 2 Chronicles 36

Seventy elders, sentries of God's law
Worship beasts and creatures slimed with blight
Weep Ezekiel, Weep for your call

Watch the Spirit flee among the tall
Cherubim, who bear Him out of sight
Hear the curse of God upon your wall
Weep you watchman, Weep for your call

Read aloud 2 Kings 23:31–25:21.

1. How does this account make you feel? _____

_____

Why? _____

_____

_____

2. Using the material just read, trace the final steps of the
   nation of Judah. _____

_____

_____

_____

_____

_____

3. a. What events in those final years make the strongest
      impression on your mind? _____

_____

_____

   b. Why do these seem especially haunting? _____

_____

_____

_____

4. In what ways might this account cause you to be more cautious in your own life? _____

_____

_____

_____

5. Use your chart to review the history of Judah. Notice particularly the names of kings, prophets, and leaders of surrounding nations. What turning points do you see that led to this kind of end? Insert a name in the first blank, then try to complete the sentence. If only _____
name

had _____

_____

_____

_____ it might have ended differently.

6. How might this study of Jewish history affect the way you pray for your own nation and its leaders? _____

_____

_____

_____

7. For what specific national needs (or leaders) ought you to be praying? _____

_____

_____

_____

_____

8. Take time now to pray together for the needs and people you have just discussed.

9. For a note of hope about Judah's future, read 2 Chronicles 6:36–39, part of Solomon's prayer for his people when he dedicated the temple. If you were to have sent a message to a person taken from Judah to Babylon, how might you have drawn from this prayer? (Try to base your message, as Solomon did, on the character of God.) ____

    _____

    _____

    _____

    _____

    _____

    _____

    _____

    _____

    _____

Read aloud 2 Chronicles 36:20–23.

10. How does this ending of the story fit what you know of God's character? _____

    _____

    _____

    _____

11. Think back over what you have learned about God through this study of Jewish history. Make one statement about God that grows out of that knowledge. _____

    _____

    _____

    _____

HELPS FOR LEADERS

1 / JEZEBEL: ENEMY TO GOD

1 Kings 21; 2 Kings 9:30–37

1. Try to involve each person present with this question.

3. Group members should notice that the public fast (symbol of mourning) drew everyone's attention to the fact that something was wrong. Jezebel seated Naboth in a prominent place so that everyone could see him. She arranged for two accusers, not just one. The accusers were to witness that Naboth had cursed both God and the king. These were each capital crimes, one on the religious front and the other in the political arena.

5. Your group should use all they have studied this far of the conflict between Ahab and Elijah. Someone may note the irony of verse 20, "So you have found me, my enemy!" Compare this with 1 Kings 18:10 and 19:3 where it was Ahab who was searching for Elijah.

6. a. The passage says Jezebel and Ahab had committed murder (v. 19); seized property (v. 19); sold themselves to do evil (vv. 20, 25); provoked God to anger (v. 22); caused Israel to sin (v. 22); Jezebel had urged Ahab on (to do evil) (v. 25); Ahab went after idols (v. 26).

b. To spur discussion of this question, you could ask, "To whom had they sold themselves?" and "What did they hope to gain from this sale?"

8. If discussion is slow on this question, consider asking, "What does Ahab's response suggest about his religious beliefs? His spiritual condition?"

10. Jezebel's name appears in the following references: 1 Kings 16:31; 18:4; 19:1–2; 21:5, 7, 11, 14–15, 23, 25; 2 Kings 9:7, 10, 22, 30, 36–37.

Use these references for your own study to be sure that your group covers the major areas. If they overlook something important in Jezebel's life, point them to the reference where it appears. But don't take time to look them all up during your discussion.

If time is short, summarize the information here, and move on to the next questions. Leave fifteen minutes for questions 11–13.

11. Your group may think this question far-fetched at first. (No one present has murdered a man for his vegetable garden.) But we, too, can oppose God. Help them look at the areas of Jezebel's opposition, then speak of similar areas of conflict today. The ideas below are listed to help you see the kind of thinking you should engender.

—Jezebel killed prophets. We could damage the reputation of a pastor or teacher. We could discourage a spiritual leader.

—Jezebel failed to learn from the Mount Carmel experience. We might choose not to respond to teachings of Scripture. We might not take advantage of opportunities to worship regularly. We might fail to show respect for God's power by refusing to obey Him.

—Jezebel stole a vineyard. We might steal time, an idea, a reputation.

—Jezebel plotted Naboth's death. We too might plot selfish revenge, but simply choose a more subtle form.

—Jezebel demanded Naboth's property. We could demand any number of things at someone else's expense: *my* favorite vacation spot; *my* television show; *my* time to be used for *my* interests.

—Jezebel urged Ahab to do evil. We may put financial pressure on a husband so that he may make questionable moral decisions in order to get the material things we want. Or we may fill his time so completely with household demands that he has no time for spiritual growth.

12. The obvious threat, as portrayed in the Jezebel story, is: "If you opposed God, He's gonna zap you." But your group should also discuss some of the more subtle dangers. For example, opposing God raises the possibility that we could eventually sell ourselves to do evil (as Ahab and Jezebel did). We would thereby lose control over our moral choices.

Your group should also notice the harm that comes to us and those close to us because of our wrong choices. God's laws are given as a kindness. They are rules by which our lives can function harmoniously. To oppose God, quite naturally, brings us harm.

13. If your group has done a thorough job with questions 11 and 12, you may omit this question.

2 / AHAB: DEAF TO GOD

1 Kings 22:1–40

1. Spend only five minutes or so on this question. The meat of the study is further on.

2. Find Ramoth Gilead on your map (p. 19). Notice that it was on or near a major trade route.

3. Spend only three or four minutes reviewing this chapter. Perhaps someone who completed the "Preparing for Study" assignment for lesson 1 will be familiar enough with the chapter to offer a brief summary.

In answer to part b, your group should know that Ahab was sullen and angry because the prophet had warned him that sparing the life of Ben-Hadad, king of Aram, would eventually cost his own life (20:41–43).

4. Your character list should include: Ahab, Jehoshaphat, Zedekiah, a messenger, 400 prophets, Micaiah, and the Lord.

6. If your group has trouble coming to the point, rephrase the question to ask, "What do these words reveal about God's purposes in these events?" They should notice that God was in control, even of the lying prophets. And that God had determined to send Ahab to his death by this means.

8. See especially verses 13–14, 24, and 26–27.

9. With this question, begin to move the discussion into a twentieth-century framework.

12. If time permits, take a brief look back at Elijah's prophecy to Ahab after the death of Naboth (21:17–19).

13. a. Question 1 will have already provided a framework for this question, so your answers here need not be exhaustive.

14, 15. Pace your study so that about ten minutes remain for these application questions.

3 / JEHOSHAPHAT: BATTLE WEARY

2 Chronicles 20:1–21:3

1. b. Your group should point out several ways that Jehoshaphat responded to the problem.

2. a. Praise occurs throughout the prayer, but several forms are found in verse 6.

b. See especially verses 7–10.

7. Don't attempt to be all-inclusive as your group discusses this question. Just spend five minutes or so pointing out both strengths and weaknesses, then move on to the next question.

While it is not included in the reading, someone may notice the ominous portent for the future in 21:4.

8, 9. Ask someone who did the "Preparing for Study" lesson to draw answers from 2 Chronicles 19. Add these to observations from chapter 20. Others may recall events from previous reading where Jehoshaphat was a secondary character. His life was interwoven with Ahab's and Jezebel's. He figures in 1 Kings 22, 2 Kings 3 and 8, and 2 Chronicles 17 through 21. Don't take time to review all of these passages now, but encourage people to discuss anything they remember from them.

12. Use information from all of Jehoshaphat's life, but be sure the discussion at this point in the study focuses on applications to the present—not to the ancient times of Jehoshaphat.

Those who did the preparatory lesson might talk about ways we can judge righteously as explained in chapter 19.

4 / ELISHA: PICKING UP THE MANTLE

2 Kings 2

1. This story raises many questions, some of them unanswerable. Encourage several people to express these questions. You could discuss some of them briefly, but don't expect to come to a consensus. Table most of the questions; you may come closer to reasonable answers as you work through the study.

2. Use the map on page 19.

The prophets apparently visited schools of prophets along the way, perhaps to give Elijah a chance to say good-by or to give final instructions or to call them together to witness the event. Your group may come up with additional ideas.

3. The text does not give definite answers to these questions, but it does supply some clues. Help your group base its opinions on these clues.

6. Your group should use the actions described in verse 12 to interpret thoughts and feelings.

Some group members may express incredulity at God's method of taking Elijah home. You could point out that this is not an isolated instance in Scripture. Prior to Elijah we read of Enoch (Genesis 5:24) and Moses (Deuteronomy 34:1–6). And the New Testament predicts similar events for believers near the end of time (1 Corinthians 15:51–52 and 1 Thessalonians 4:15–18).

If your group wants to play with this idea for a bit, you could ask, "If you could choose between death and this alternate ending to life on earth, which would you prefer? Why?"

7. Group members should point out the following quotations: "The LORD has sent," "As the LORD lives," "The LORD is going to take." They might also point out the actions of the divided water, the whirlwind, the fiery horses and chariot.

8. a. Don't spend undue time here; just let your group mention several events from memory, then move to the next question.

12. Of the rather alarming incident of the youths and the bears, we should note that Elisha did not kill them; he only cursed them. Evidently God brought out the bears in response. Keil and Delitzsch say that this was "Intended to prove to the despisers of God that the Lord does not allow his servants to be ridiculed with impunity" (p. 299).

In addition, since Elisha served as prophet in Israel for another fifty years, it is not likely that he was actually bald at this time.

For a fun question, if you have extra time, try, "Would you like to have Elisha living in your town? Why, or why not?"

13. Omit this question if you are short of time. Be sure to leave time for the personal questions at the end.

14, 15. Pace your study so that you have at least ten minutes left to discuss questions 14 and 15.

Everyone ought to be able to think of one job that God has given them to do. General assignments might include: to raise my children in a spiritually and emotionally healthy way; to be a good wife to my husband; to work for my employer honestly and with diligence.

More specialized answers might include: to be a writer who brings honor and glory to God; to teach Sunday school; to work on the school board in a way that is fair to the entire community.

When you have heard several answers to question 14, move on to question 15 and develop those responses more fully.

5 / ELISHA: FAITH IN HARD TIMES

2 Kings 6:24–7:20

1. The cannibalism is, of course, the most shocking evidence. But your group should comb the passage for some eight to ten other indications.

4. Your group should pick out the king's comments in verses 27, 31, and 33; Elisha's in 7:1; the officer's in 7:2. Don't settle for a simple repetition of the words, but discuss the implied belief (or lack of belief) behind those words. If they are slow to take this extra step, ask more specific questions such as, "What did the officer believe about God; what did he not believe?"

8. a. Call up the details of verses 13–15.

b. See especially verses 12–13.

10. Linger here long enough to engage in meaningful discussion. Some may not like the view of God presented here. Others may not agree with it. But disasters do occur. God is either sovereign over disasters, as well as the lovely and good, or He is not an all-powerful God.

Of the characters in the story, the king acknowledged that God was still in control, but he expected nothing good (for him) to come of it. Elisha knew God was in charge, and he could promise relief because of God's word to him as a prophet. Only the officer saw God's authority as limited— and he died.

12. Don't encourage intimacy beyond a reasonable comfort level for your group. Only a few need to speak of their "disasters" for the whole group to benefit, if these few speak honestly and to the point.

13. Those who did not speak of personal disasters could contribute here. Someone should remember the large scope of God's authority that today's passage assumes. If we can become convinced of this in the good times, it may sustain us when times are rough.

6 / JEHU: GOD'S AVENGER

2 Kings 9–10

1. Include as many group members as possible in responding to this question. Don't attempt to solve all of the dilemmas this passage poses. Just acknowledge that it's reasonable to feel confused and angry about it.

2. a. See 9:3–7. Notice that the directions to Jehu are nonspecific: He is to "destroy the house of Ahab." Regarding the list of actions of verses 7–10, God says that He Himself will do it. Did Jehu overstep his instructions with the mass executions? Or did God simply choose to do what He said He would do through Jehu?

b. See 9:1–3.

3. a. Second Kings 9:9 refers to Baasha and Jeroboam. For each family, your group should note what happened, how, and why. This passage also explains Jezebel's reference to Zimri in 2 Kings 9:31. (See 1 Kings 16:12.) The old queen knew what was happening beneath her tower.

d. Notice several reasons in verses 17–29. Then glance back over the chapter if necessary to remember the events surrounding Naboth's vineyard. Be sure that someone points out the reason for the delay of God's judgment on Ahab (vv. 27–29). They should also notice the place prophesied for judgment. (Compare 1 Kings 21:19 with 2 Kings 9:21–26.)

4. Find Jehu (9:1–2), Joram (9:15), Ahaziah (9:16), and Jezebel (9:30).

5. Help your group list these in order by noting the reference for each.

Joram (9:24)

Ahaziah (9:27) (Even though he was king of Judah, he was Ahab's grandson by marriage. See 2 Kings 8:18, 25, 27.)

Jezebel (9:33)

70 sons of the house of Ahab (10:7)

all Ahab's chief men (10:11)

all his close friends (10:11)

all his priests (10:11)

42 relatives of Ahaziah (10:14)

all who were left of Ahab's family in Samaria (10:17)

all the prophets, ministers, and priests of Baal (10:21–25)

6. b. Possible answers might be drawn from 9:18–20; 9:32–33; 10:1–5; 10:9; 10:18–24.

7. See 10:28–31 as well as the political motives outlined by the other events here.

8. The repeated summary of each king, "And he did good/evil in the sight of the LORD," is missing for Jehu. Your group ought to be able to defend either answer. Even God's response to his reign is mixed. (See 2 Kings 10:30–33.) No need to expect a consensus.

9. Your findings in response to question 3 will be especially helpful here. Use these, but draw on any other information from the passage.

10. This is a question that has plagued serious thinkers for centuries. Some have even turned away from faith because of it. Some say, "God is *not* good; therefore I do not wish to serve Him." Or, conversely, "God is not sovereign. There are forces of evil beyond His control. Even I may step beyond His control." Those who say this assume that God is less than God and wonder why they should worship a being who is not supreme.

A more orthodox view says, "God is good and God is

sovereign, but He has chosen to relinquish control over certain situations." For example, He allows people to choose for or against moral behavior and for or against salvation. God gives them over to their own choices. To support this view, Romans 1:24–32 uses the phrase "God gave them over" three times.

But today's passage does not seem to speak of evil freely chosen in contradiction to the will of God. Here we see Jehu ordered by God to "destroy" the house of Ahab; so Jehu proceeded systematically to exterminate everyone related to Ahab, even though this included more than a hundred people. True, Jehu may have had his own reasons for these executions. And true, we do not see him as a particularly godly man; yet God used him for the larger purpose of ridding His people of an evil influence.

It is this possibility of a larger, often unseen, purpose that can keep us clinging to faith in the face of violent newspaper headlines. We do not need to condone the violence. But neither do we need to assume that just because we cannot see His purpose, God has abdicated His throne. Even Jehu probably did not see the divine purpose in what he was doing. (He had his own ax to grind.) And the ordinary street worker in Samaria certainly didn't. But God was still in charge. This story can help us believe in God—even when violence shakes our world.

Discussion of this question will grow out of the objections raised in question 1. If the group has done a thorough job today, it should now have some solutions to the objections expressed when the study opened. But the subject is not easy. So don't expect simple solutions or total agreement.

Note: A well-trained Bible student may point out Hosea 1:4, written about one hundred years later, where God says, "I will soon punish the house of Jehu for the massacre at

Jezreel." God used Jehu to rid Israel of Ahab's ungodly influence. But Jehu's violence does not pass unjudged.

7 / JOASH: PROTÉGÉ TO A PRIEST

2 Chronicles 23–24

1. Your group should point out, in sequence, the steps of Jehoiada's thorough groundwork. Those who worked on the "Preparing for Study" section can add the background found in 22:10–12.

2. See verses 1–3 and 11 to discover with whom the covenant was made.

4. Let your group discuss this for a few moments. If they seem confused, ask them to look at Leviticus 19:30 for a command from God that might have some bearing on the event. (Hold this information in your mind; it will also relate to discussion of question 11.)

5. Find six or more actions in verses 16–20.

6. If you think you will have extra time, ask, "Why do you think the people responded the way they did to this change in leadership?" (See v. 21.)

7. Linger on this question long enough to wrap up all the information given thus far. Don't neglect the summary given in 24:2–3.

8. b. Several answers grow out of verses 6–9.

9. Notice the balances of authority in the details of verses 8–14.

11. Include Joash's change in spiritual direction (vv. 17–22) as well as the political effects on the people (vv. 23–27).

12. Notice the purpose of the prophets in verse 19. Notice also the death of Zechariah, Jehoiada's son, who may have been raised as a brother to Joash. Notice also the job assigned to the prophets and the setting in which they had to perform that work.

14, 15. Ask each of your group members to select *one* of these two questions, then spend a couple of minutes silently making notes about it. Share several responses.

8 / HAZAEL: AN ENEMY TO MAKE PROPHETS WEEP

2 Kings 13

1. Your group should cite eight or ten details from these verses.

2. It will help your group members to answer this if they can spot the connective phrases between actions: "He did" (v. 2), "So" (v. 3), "Then" (v. 4), "The Lord provided" (v. 5), "But" (v. 6).

3. This enigmatic statement could have several meanings. Possible interpretations include: Elisha was worth all of the chariots and horses of Israel; Jehoash was mourning the loss of the country's chariots and horses (v. 7); "Your chariot and horses are coming as they did for Elijah" (2 Kings 2:12) ("You are about to die. Will you have chariots and horses as Elijah did?").

Your group may think of these or other possible interpretations. It will aid the discussion if you encourage people to tell why they interpret the statement the way they do.

6. See verses 20–21.

7. a. Be sure that you have at least half of your time left when you begin question 7.

b. Elisha was carrying out a command originally given to

Elijah, part of the mantle he picked up after Elijah's departure.

10. Your group should here refer to the maps. If Hazael marched from Damascus through all the territory east of Jordan, then on to Gath and was threatening Jerusalem, little was left but a small section of Samaria. Even Judah, to the south, was in trouble.

If your time is short, summarize the answer to this and go on to question 11.

At the close of the study, ask your group to look at the "Preparing for Study" section for the coming week. You are entering the era of Israel's history where prophets played a major role; you will begin to study some of the prophets alongside the kings, thus making longer preparatory lessons. Next week's preparation includes an unusual amount of reading. Suggest that they start it early in the week.

9 / ISAIAH: PROPHET OF VISION

Isaiah 6

3. If answers are incomplete, break this question into three parts.

    a. How did Isaiah respond to what he had seen?

    b. How did God respond to Isaiah?

    c. How did Isaiah respond to God?

4. "Unclean" appears twice in verse 5.

5. Let your group discuss this for a few moments. They will probably come to a solution similar to that expressed in *New Bible Commentary*, p. 595:

> The fiery messenger and burning coal must have presaged at first anything but salvation . . . ; yet they came

from the place of sacrifice and spoke the language of atonement. . . . The *burning coal* symbolizes the total significance of the altar from which it came; that the penalty of sin was paid by a substitute offered in the sinner's place. The symbol, applied to Isaiah's lips, the point at which his need was most pressing, assures him of personal forgiveness.

6. b. Your group should have several answers; among them should be the fact that God hadn't even revealed *where* He intended to send Isaiah!

7. a. and b. Consider treating these two questions together, since they are so closely related.

8. Notice the people (vv. 9–10) and the events (vv. 11–13). *New Bible Commentary* comments on verse 10:

Isaiah fulfilled this commission to blind and deafen by proclaiming (not withholding) the truth. . . . Sinful Israel has come to the point where one more rejection of the truth will finally confirm them for inevitable judgment. The dilemma of the prophet is that there is no way of saving the sinner but by the very truth whose rejection will condemn him utterly (p. 595).

10. Some groups could spend all of their remaining time on this question. Discuss it long enough to touch on the major issues, but save enough time to do justice to the rest of the study.

10 / AHAZ: FAITHLESS IN TROUBLE

2 Kings 16

4. Ahaz must have been inspecting the aqueduct for his city's water supply after the siege against Jerusalem (2 Kings 16:5) in preparation for another siege.

5. a. verses 6–7

b. verses 9–11

c. verse 12

6. Your group may think of any number of reasons. Just be sure they do not conflict with information in either of the two passages you have studied. Several possibilities are hinted at there.

8. Check the map for changes in the Assyrian borders. By forming an alliance with the most dangerous nation in the area, Ahaz had brought Assyrian borders to his own doorstep. Group members should also notice, in verse 9, the treatment a conquered nation could expect from Assyria. Ahaz has also been guilty, before God, of turning his sister nation (Israel) over to a common enemy. Participants may find other reasons that grow out of the passage.

12. a. and b. This question is for personal reflection, not discussion. So read aloud part a, leave time to write, then read aloud part b, and again allow time to write. Then go on to question 13.

13. a. Group members should respond to these questions in a way that fits their own troublesome situations. Possible attempts to find "other gods and other altars" in the sample situations might include: I would leave my church that is in turmoil; I would stop praying for a while when my friend dies; I would express excessive anger at my husband, assuming that he, not God, is to take care of me; I would put *all* my faith in counseling as an aid to my parents, not putting it in its proper perspective as one of the gifts from a living God who hates divorce.

11 / HOSHEA: IDOLATRY'S REWARD

2 Kings 17

1. Invite everyone present to answer this question in some way. Ask several to explain why they feel the way they do.

2. Someone may point out the apparent time discrepancy between 2 Kings 15:30 and 17:1. In their *Old Testament Commentaries,* Keil and Delitzsch explain this by suggesting that in this turbulent era an eight-year period of anarchy probably occurred before Hoshea was able to secure the throne (p. 409).

3. See the details of verses 1−6 as well as verse 24. Along with the other details, notice that Assyria imprisoned the Israeli king, captured the people of Israel, deported them to a land some six hundred miles away, and spread out the Jews so they could not form a cohesive group. To make sure there would be no vacant land to invite a return, Assyria, at the same time, imported other peoples to Samaria and settled them there. Second Chronicles 30:5−11 and 34:6−9 suggest that a few Jews escaped deportation, but even these must have mingled with the imported groups and so lost any Jewish identity.

5. If your group seems sensitive to this, you can also ask, "What would being removed from the presence of God mean to you?"

9. These events help us understand the New Testament animosity between the Jews and the Samaritans because they help define the historic roots of the Samaritan people.

(Remember Jesus' encounter with the Samaritan woman in John 4?) See the mixture described in 2 Kings 17:24 as well as the hint of a few remaining Jews in 2 Chronicles 30:5–11.

These events also explain the later controversy over place of worship. The priest sent to Samaria reestablished worship (probably a paganized version of Jewish worship) at Bethel, a place Jeroboam had designed for worship during the initial civil war to prevent his people from crossing the border to worship in Jerusalem and perhaps defecting to Judah in the South (1 Kings 12:25–33). But southern Jews insisted, quite correctly, that Jerusalem was the only proper place for God's temple.

12. Allow a few moments of silence for each person to make notes here. (Be prepared with extra pencils.) Then go on to question 13.

13, 14. Save five or ten minutes for these final application questions. Encourage several to respond as honestly as is practical. After others have spoken, be ready to share some of your own thinking on the subject.

12 / HEZEKIAH: KING IN CRISIS

Isaiah 36–37

1. Find Lachish on the map. (It is *south* of Jerusalem, indicating that Assyria was already in charge of much Judean territory.) Notice the three men representing King Hezekiah and the field commander representing the king of Assyria. "The Upper Pool, on the road to the Washerman's Field" (v. 2) is the same one where Isaiah had met King Ahaz (Isaiah 7:3). It was the source of the city's water supply. Hezekiah, however, sometime during his reign built an alternate source for water. (See 2 Chronicles 32:2—4, 30 and 2 Kings 20:20.)

3. Find twisted truth throughout the passage. Your group should touch on the ways he tried to undermine their faith in political allies (Egypt), their faith in King Hezekiah, their faith in God.

4. If you have extra time, ask also: "If you had been King Hezekiah, newly informed about this meeting, what would you have done?"

7. The military movements of Egypt brought renewed Assyrian ire on Hezekiah. Your group should notice the spiritual threats behind this new warning from Sennacherib.

Note: Did Sennacherib wage one campaign against Jerusalem or two? There is no easy answer. For a thorough treatment of the problem read John Bright's *A History of Israel,* pages 298—309.

8. Allow enough time for your group to examine the high quality of worship in Hezekiah's prayer, though Hezekiah did not deny the critical circumstances he faced. Even so, his purpose for requesting help was an evangelistic vindication of God's character: "So that all kingdoms on earth may know that you alone, O LORD, are God" (v. 20).

9. Your group should find divisions and titles similar to these:

God's people (v. 22)
God's holiness (v. 23)
God's enemies (vv. 24—25)
God's sovereignty (vv. 26—27)
God's knowledge (v. 28)
God's power (v. 29)
God's redemption (vv. 33—34)
God's reasons (v. 35)

10. Your group should find many ways in which this story attacks the Assyrian accusations. There is particular irony in comparing Isaiah 36:10 "The LORD himself told me to march against this country and destroy it," with 37:26–27. The Assyrian's words were more true than he realized; yet God would turn that same sovereign power back on the Assyrians. (See v. 29.)

Your group may also notice the irony of the Assyrian question, "On whom are you depending?" (36:5), when viewed in light of the whole thrust of this song, "Whom have you mocked?"

If you have time for additional questions try, "Compare verses 26–27 with the Assyrian taunt of 36:10. In what ways was the field commander correct? How was his perspective limited?"

Or for a more personal tack ask, "How might this song help you to worship God?"

13 / MANASSEH: ONE GIANT STEP BACKWARD

2 Kings 20–21

1. Your group should find many details in these verses that show what kind of relationship they had.

There is no hint in this passage that it was inappropriate for Hezekiah to request a sign. In Isaiah 7:10–12, Ahaz was invited by God to request a sign. (He refused but got one anyway.)

Did the earth stop in its orbit and turn backward? "Not likely," say most commentators. *New Bible Commentary* is typical of much scholarly opinion: "Whether the sun was actually moved backward, or some refraction of its rays caused its shadow to move backward, is a discussion based

on attempts to find more than the biblical text actually says"
(p. 364).

2. Hezekiah may have had any number of reasons, some
admirable, some not:

He may have wanted a political alliance with natural
enemies of Assyria.

He may have been exhibiting pride in his possessions.
(Second Chronicles 32:25–26 suggests this.)

He may have wanted to show trust and honor to messengers from royalty.

Use your map to find geographic relationships between
Assyria, Babylon, and Judah.

6. Notice the quote of the promise given to the people
during Solomon's dedication of the temple, and the conditions (for the people) attached to it (vv. 7–8).

Verse 9 says the *people* did not listen.

Verse 15 sums up God's view of the actions of His people.
Notice that this is in no way limited to the era of Manasseh.

7. Notice the symbol of the plumb line (also mentioned in
Amos 7:7 as a prophecy against the northern kingdom); the
wiped dish; the term *remnant;* the ominous references to
Samaria (whose people already were deported to Assyria);
and the house of Ahab. Remember Jehu?

9. Note on verse 16: "Josephus . . . says that Manasseh
slew some every day. According to tradition he slew Isaiah
the prophet, sawing him asunder" (*New Bible Commentary*,
p. 365).

11. This question is not as straightforward as it seems.
True, Manasseh was born in that fifteen years, but prior to
that, Hezekiah had fathered no sons—and so his death
would have ended a 250-year line of Davidic kings.

In addition, by comparing 18:2, 13, and 20:6, we find that
Hezekiah's illness must have occurred just *prior* to the siege

of Sennacherib. If he had died during that illness, he would have left the throne vacant at a critical time.

Sharp-eyed readers may notice that the text does not say that Hezekiah asked for an extension to his life. God simply responded to his tearful prayer by giving it.

12. No easy answer fits here. Your group may think of possible solutions such as:

—God simply let the people follow their natural bent since their days in Egypt (21:15).

—God allowed Manasseh to prolong the life of the nation by not making waves with strong pagan enemies.

—God had already decided to judge the nation and simply used Manasseh as an instrument toward that end.

—God wanted to test and strengthen any remaining true believers.

Note: Second Chronicles 33:10–17 records a period of personal reform during Manasseh's reign (probably near the end of his life), but verse 17 reflects little change in the practices of the people.

If time is short, treat this question only briefly and conserve time for the final two questions of application.

14 / JOSIAH: BOY KING; ADULT REFORMER

2 Kings 22:1–23:30

Note: If you want to conduct a rather thorough discussion of what makes up a godly response to God's law, treat the early questions of the study briefly and reserve time for questions 11–14, delving into the additional questions suggested in questions 12–13 of these Helps. Or if you have an extra week in your agenda, you might split the study after question 8.

1. See the details of 22:1–8.

3. a. See verse 14.

b. Base the answers on verses 15–20.

5. Note on verse 22: Hezekiah also celebrated Passover as part of his reform. (See 2 Chronicles 30.) But Hezekiah did not have the benefit of specific instructions for Passover from the Book of the Law. And his animal sacrifices were only one tenth of those recorded for Josiah. Second Chronicles 35:7 states that the sacrificial animals came from Josiah's own possessions.

Note on verse 17: "The man of God who came from Judah." Review 1 Kings 13 for an interesting sidelight of personal study.

8. If you want to divide this study in half to spread it over two sessions, end the first discussion after question 8.

9. Draw on the prophets read during "Preparing for Study" as well as 2 Kings 22:15–20 and 23:26–27.

This question may be omitted if you want to emphasize the last section.

10. Skip this question, or summarize it briefly if you are short of time.

11. If the question of New Testament law versus Old Testament Law comes into the discussion in this or a later question, you could comment that Old Testament Law is often divided into three categories: ceremonial law, civil law, and moral law. New Testament Christians need only be bound by the moral law of the Old Testament. But segregating what is moral law from the other two categories is no small task.

12. If you want the discussion to take a more personal direction, ask, "Think back on your own responses to God's law. Try to think of a specific standard of behavior that you became aware of rather suddenly. What were your first feelings about that law?''

For an alternate question or a follow-up question ask, ''Why is the term 'law,' even if it belongs to God, hard for us to live with?''

For another follow-up question, ask, ''What advantage is it to the believer to have a system of behavior prescribed by God?''

13. If time permits ask also, ''What does the fact that God sets standards of behavior for His people reveal about the character of God?''

15 / ZEDEKIAH: END OF THE LINE

2 Kings 23:31–25:21

2. Help your group tell in sequence the outline of events recorded here.

3. a. and b. Treat these two questions simultaneously.

5. The godly kings Hezekiah and Josiah, each followed by sons who took the nation away from God, are almost certain to come up. Of these, *New Bible Commentary* asks: ''We must ask ourselves, Why? Hezekiah forgot to ask the LORD before he opened his treasury to the Babylonians, and Josiah forgot to ask whether he should go to Megiddo—is there any connection?'' (p. 366).

9. Work with this question either through discussion or by having each person write a message, then read it to the group.

11. Encourage a brief sentence of response from each person present.

BIBLIOGRAPHY

Aharoni, Yohanan, and Michael Avi-Yonah. *The Macmillan Bible Atlas*. New York: Macmillan, 1977.

Alexander, David, and Pat Alexander, eds. *Eerdmans' Handbook to the Bible*. Grand Rapids: Eerdmans, 1973.

Bright, John. *A History of Israel*. 3d ed. Philadelphia: Westminster Press, 1981.

Douglas, J. D., ed. *The New Bible Dictionary*. Grand Rapids: Eerdmans, 1962.

Edersheim, Alfred. *Old Testament Bible History*. Grand Rapids: Eerdmans, 1979.

Guthrie, D., J. A. Motyer, A. M. Stibbs, and D. J. Wiseman. *New Bible Commentary*. Rev. ed. Grand Rapids: Eerdmans, 1970.

Harrison, Roland Kenneth. *A History of Old Testament Times*. London: Marshall, Morgan, and Scott, 1957.

Keil, C. F., and F. Delitzsch. *Old Testament Commentaries*. Grand Rapids: Eerdmans. Reprinted 1980.

Pfeiffer, Charles F. *An Outline of Old Testament History*. Chicago: Moody Press, 1975.

Roberts, David. *Yesterday the Holy Land*. Translated by Ed van der Maas. Grand Rapids: Zondervan, 1982.

Schultz, Samuel J. *The Old Testament Speaks*. New York: Harper & Brothers, 1960.

Tenney, Merrill C., gen. ed. *The Zondervan Pictorial Encyclopedia of the Bible*. Grand Rapids: Zondervan, 1975.

Thiele, Edwin R. *A Chronology of the Hebrew Kings*. Grand Rapids: Zondervan, 1977.

_____. *The Mysterious Numbers of the Hebrew Kings*. Grand Rapids: Eerdmans, 1951.

INDEX